T H E

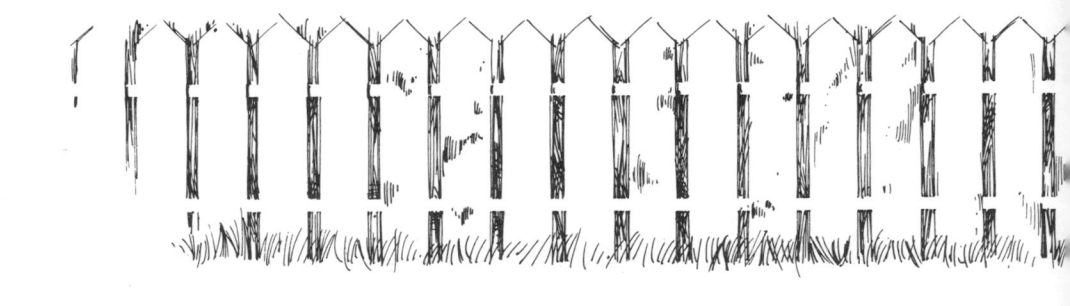

GREETING

New & Selected Poems

R. H.W. Dillard

University of Utah Press
Salt Lake City
1981

UNIVERSITY OF UTAH PRESS POETRY SERIES
DAVE SMITH, *Editor*

Some of the poems in "The Greeting" and "January: A Screenplay"
have appeared in the following places: *The Black Warrior Review, Jeopardy,
The Nantucket Review, Vanderbilt Poetry Review, Two Dam Poems.*
These publishers have graciously allowed inclusion of a number of poems
from the following collections: The University of North Carolina Press,
The Day I Stopped Dreaming About Barbara Steele (1966) and
News of the Nile (1971); and Louisiana State University Press,
After Borges (1972).

Library of Congress Cataloguing in Publication Data

Dillard, R. H. W. (Richard H. W.), 1937–
    The greeting.

    (University of Utah Press poetry series)
    I. Title.   II. Series.
PS3554.I4G7   811'.54   81-16143
ISBN 0-87480-200-8   AACR2

For Cathy

Prayer of the lover, this prayer,
Lover and lover

BOOKS BY R. H. W. DILLARD

POETRY

The Day I Stopped Dreaming About Barbara Steele
and Other Poems, 1966

News of the Nile: A Book of Poems, 1971

After Borges: A Sequence of New Poems, 1972

The Greeting: New & Selected Poems, 1981

FICTION

The Book of Changes, 1974

CRITICISM

Horror Films, 1976

CONTENTS

THE GREETING

THE GREETING

Hello. It is like an echo
Of something I have always known:
From a bush (where you are burning),
From a cloud (you are alone),
The stream's dry whisper, river's slide,
Stone, thistle, the startling leap
Of a jewel weed. I always know the voice.
It is one day hers; one day, his.
Today it is yours.

Hello. And the leaves lapse
Into applause, a flight of monarchs
Dizzies and stills, the high stone arch
Coos with a flutter of doves.
It is like a breeze I have always felt,
Billowing out the silent curtains,
Bumping the pictures on the walls.
One day it is a warm breeze; one day, cold.
Today it is you.

Hello. It is like the face
Of someone I have always known:
The smile of recognition, frown of fear,
Snarl that splits it like a shell,
Blank face of the dreamer, silent dream.
I have always known the dream,
How it lights and flares, how it fades.
It is one day mine; one day, yours.
It is today.

WALKING WITH YOUNG WOMEN

The evening air less warm than blood,
A sense of grass, hills of grass and white cows,
Mountains of grass, seas of grass,
New mown or still growing, and the sun's demise.

Walking with young women,
She has taken off her shoes,
The gravels hurt her white bare feet,
There are tiny brown feet on the sleeve
Of her shirt, on the roadway, in the grass,
She has a butterfly on her blouse,
Walking with young women
Between white fences, fields of grass,
The random cat (white and black).

In the stables the enormous horses
Nuzzle the backs of young women,
The blazes of their heads fiercely white,
She remembers riding one when she was three,
While she walks over to her own horse,
The roan stallion with the gray in his mane,
She swats at a fly, she pats the spotted dog
(Black on white), she stoops to see the shaggy hooves.

Walking with young women after sunset
When the air is cooling slowly
And the grass settles back into itself,
Green on green, the air easing to gray,
Your hair gray at the temples, going white,
Walking between white fences,
Walking with young women as in a dream,
As in memory, as in fact,
Walking with young women down the long hill
Past the clipped green grass of the lawns
As electric lights stammer on
And the day dawdles down into night.

AT THE FOOT OF THE DAM

for Dara Wier

The blood catches in your ear,
That soft pump still,
The rain rolling its own dark rhythm
On the tin roof, on the swollen ground,
The creek moaning like an injured bear
Or a hound torn one last time to earth.

The phone draws you from sleep
Like water from a well. It is the sheriff.
He is calling to tell you the dam is weak,
The stone stiff and sore and bruised,
The shoulders of the hills begun to slump.
They are old hills. It is an aging dam.

The rain drowns his busy voice,
Or maybe the wires are down.

And then it cracks. The dam
Splits like a snake's back or the shell
Of a crab. The air opens to it.
The lake splashes through like a new plant,
The wet fat leaves splashing into the night,
Rising like a plume, a desperately heavy fern.

The house jumps like a startled cat,
It rattles, lurches, weaves across the lawn,
Begins to bounce like water on a hot stone.

You are riding the river, dancing on water,
Swimming in air, filling the narrow valley
As sound may fill an empty music hall,
Foot and heel and toe, wet waltz,
Wild saraband, an eastern hoedown.

What a way to start the day.

But you are not surprised, nor will be the sun.
Nothing so new after all,
Just life at the foot of the dam.

DREAM-LAND, LANDSCAPE LIKE A DREAM

for Lucette Bernard

It is more real than anything you have ever seen.

It is less real.

It is a mountain hung and looming
So high you must bend back to see,
So close you must bend back to see,
The low clouds moving slow and still and grey,
Grey green of spruce and pine, needles
Wet and glowing, water skims the wooden rails,
The cabin walls, wet and close and grey and glowing.

You see it more clearly than you have ever seen a thing.

You see it in a haze, a mist, a blur.

The wall that bends, the door that slams,
Window through which he crawls, knee on the sill,
The slanting sidewalk down which she strolls,
The river, curling stream,
Familiar hill that you have only seen
The once before, that you have never seen,
Loose ground through which the acorns crawl.

It is still and more stable than anything you have ever known.

It moves like oil, sliding on still water.

It is a ceiling that spreads, that disappears,
Locked door that breaks into the room without a sound,
That tall, incredible, irresistible man (no eyes)
Who crosses to you faster than an eye,
He crosses you, the floor that falters,
Walls that turn and bend and close,
The light that slides on walls.

It is your hand, his, hers, our hands,
Turn of your face, uneasy silence,
The trees that bend and stagger, each valley

That floats in mountains like an echo or a pause,
It is a distance that reaches you, that touches you,
It is yourself spread far and thin,
It is a growth beyond dimension,
It is the voice that whispers in the flood,
The life that washes in your veins,
Sun's startling rise, surprising fall,
The turn of day on night on day on day.

It is more real than you have ever seen.

It is everything you ever see.

SOME LIGHT WORDS

for Cathy

How, love, in this frenzy of illuminant particles,
each atom a spark,
May I you touch?

— Fred Chappell

"Where others see objects," Tom said,
"Cathy sees light." And he's right. You do,
Articulate light, light entranced, coherent
And incoherent light, light holding hands with light,
Each object, ring and oval mirror, eye and camera's eye,
Lip, lid, and lens and circling butterfly, weather sign
And the hands' sure sign, love in the language of hands,
Each a concretion of light, light involved,
Light made sure, wave and scatter, color and blur,
Generative ring and ring and ring.

"It is my heart you hold in yours," you said,
"Two hearts in one." And you're right. I do,
Heart and linked heart, like a silver key ring,
Heart caught in heart and the key to a heart,
Your heart, mine, no need to be alone, single hand
Tracing a keyless chain, no need, no need,
For it is like my dream: the complex city,
Detailed map, the light tracing my random path
Over a shoulder until I look up and see you
In the window, and you are saying, "You are here."

"We are like shadows on the wall," I said,
"Moving as light." And I'm right. We do,
Loving in the open (your phrase), in love
With you loving (yours too), light and dark
Like held hands or locked hearts (each to each,
No one apart), day, night, dawn, dusk,
Sun's curve, moon's continuing surprise,
Star and star and star and star, planet's turn,
Ring on ring, hand and hand, heart in heart,
This touching that says love in the language of light.

JANUARY: A SCREENPLAY

The water breaks. Rain races the highway.
You see long slicks of red and yellow light
On the wet road ahead, then green and green,
And the arch and sway of electric lines
Traced in water, caught in light.

Voice Over:
"Light that opens the day of open windows."

Voice Over:
"The past dissolves in water like a year."

Voice Over:
"Receive your sight; your faith has made you well."

Clouds of fog hold to the hilltops,
And you see the headlights dazzle and disappear,
The eye grow pale. This motion through the dark,
This punctuation of light, light beam,
Light reflecting on the lines, diffuse light
In this perplexity of floating fog.

His head turns to hers.
She shows him the way.
She knows the way.
She knows when he is where he ought to be.

Time opens on this second,
Opens in, opens out, time like a fog,
Time like a play of light,
As through the window you see the rush
And play of rain across the night,
Light's venture into rain,
This opening window like an open eye.

2. INSERT: HER HANDS

Her hands:
This motion:
Her hands moving before a chainlink fence,
Moving in the shadows on a blue wall,
Shadows of trees, of branches moving,
Her hands typing a letter or tying a shoe,
Her hands carefully folding a letter,
Her hands stretching in the morning,
Finger and finger and finger and finger
And thumb,
Her hands suddenly shy,
Her hands opening with delight,
With the fruit of her hands she plants a vineyard,
She touches his face with her hand,
He holds her hand in his, both of his,
Hand and her hand and hand,
The sudden surprise as she takes his arm
As though her hands knew before he did,
As though her hands knew before she did,
Her hands making a circle, a frame
Through which the camera's eye may see.

The air looks as clear as an eye,
Cold eye, blue, eye of the sun
Set in its center, eye and eye,
Sharp and open and true.

She wears the sun's eye
On a silver chain.
He wears the sun's blind rim.
Solid eye and empty circle,
Whole when they touch, fit,
Become the single sun
Of a single sky.

You see the airplanes' tails
Against the cold blue sky,
White on blue, white on blue,
Cross and cross and cross
In graceful repetition.

You see the world cease
In this stationary air,
Wearied with the journey,
Its breath close around you
Like a clear cloud,
Blind sun, ring of mountains,
Light like silent water,
Tilt of the day.

He stands by the chainlink fence,
His gloved hands pressed against the cold,
Against the cold hard fence,
Fingers spread, his sight pressed
Against the airplane
Where she is waiting, far away.

It is just now a still life, this air,
This cold, that distance,
The man, the fence, the plane,
This sun, this suspended day,
World, sky,
This solitary moment,
This departure,
This man who holds to what he does not see.

It does move. He knows that.

He remembers a sweep of clouds
Massing and spreading over the western mountain.
He remembers the sun's arch and dive,
The great nebula's curl across the telescope,
The red and blue shimmer of rising Jupiter.
He remembers the rush of the creek's water
And the frightened screak of the killdeer
As they walked too near on the road.
He remembers the moon's turn, so timed,
And the earth's turn, and the sun's,
And the whole galaxy's slow revolution
In a turning universe. It does move.

He imagines the movement of blood
Through his still hand, imagines
Pigeons settling in distant Russell Square,
Imagines a long slow line of passengers
Moving cautiously toward the narrow gate,
Imagines that someone has just touched him,
Touched his face, imagines all the clocks
In every land speeding up, racing time
Forward and forward, hears her voice
Speak his name three times, imagines
Her voice, his name. It does move.

He sees only the still cold sky,
No slice or sliver of drifting cloud,
The brittle grass and the sloping lawn,
Silent tree and empty birdfeeder,
The creek lying low, edged with rime,
The empty road, nothing going by,
Nothing going on. He sees nothing.

And in this silence, gone away from there,
Gone away from here, nowhere,
His eyes empty as the sightless sun,
He hears a voice, his own,
Telling her name on his tongue
Like a prayer.

5. EXT. THE MOUNTAIN DAY

He remembers:

The long fall light,
The early November air, bright up ahead,
The shift and shatter of leaves on the trail,
The crashing dog's rough passage up and back,
The broken trees and long-split stone,
The mountain and the sun's lost afternoon.

She is wearing her camera,
He is waving his walking stick,
These two friends in their identical shoes,
Suddenly shy, suddenly talking together,
Suddenly climbing this mountain in the autumn woods.

Voice Over:
"Unless you see signs and wonders you will not believe."

They start upon a deer
Near the top of the rattling trail,
Tossed on its neck, the hair smooth as light,
Already round with sure decay,
Laid out in the day's last turning
As token, as warning, as wonder, as sign.

Voice Over:
"The mountain opens and admits you to light."

At the mountain's top,
Standing on ridge rock, looking out to the sunset
Across the flat reflecting cove far below,
She takes his picture as he looks away,
And around his head a nimbus, aureole,
Halo, echo of sunlight over distant water.

Voice Over:
"Light that opens the day of open windows."

And as they descend into the swelling dark,
From stone to slick shale, to leaf and fallen tree,

He hears a shadow of wings, light's shadow,
The angel that speaks the word and bears the gift,
Although he does not yet know to know.

He only knows that they are walking together,
That they have seen signs and wonders,
That the new evening deepens like water,
That the leaves spill around their feet,
That if he took her hand
He would never let it go.

He is driving alone
Through light rain and wisps of winter fog,
The shirr of the tires,
Slick slap of the windshield wiper.

Over his shoulder you see the blurred day,
A truck's explosive passing,
The smear and slide across the glass,
The nearly empty streets, random cars,
Two children tilted under a single umbrella,
Their yellow slickers catching what light there is,
Giving it back in a glint across the water,
His hands on the wheel, holding it lightly,
Drifting with the road's drift,
Angling into turns, a finger snapping the turn signal
On, tapping it off when the bend's too slight.
You hear its tick and tick, the clock's small whir,
The steady engine, rain's rap on the roof.

The rain, this driving in the rain,
Renews him like a sparrow, like a hawk,
Lifts him, helps him to remember,
Helps him to imagine, helps him to know
Just who will satisfy him,
As long as he lives, with good.

He reaches to the radio,
And the car fills with music,
A wash of music from window to window
To window to window,
The guitar, the piano, voices, words,
Seen a face, across the water, dying day,
Though he scarcely hears it.
He is far away.

The car rushes into deeper water,
Windows slurred as the day disappears,
Until you see it lift and plunge,
Lunge out and sail on wings of water,
On wings of air.

7. INSERT: THE POSTCARD

It is a Magritte,
La grande famille, the big family,
This bird of sky, a prayer of angles,
Over rolling water, against lowering clouds,
This bird of air and white cloud,
Its head the same as the stone bird's head
In *Le domaine d'Arnheim* of 1949,
Its head not the same as the stone bird's head
In *Le domaine d'Arnheim* of 1962,
This bird through which you see
What you can see.

Voice Over:
"A thing which is present can be invisible,
 Hidden by what it shows."

Voice Over:
"The creation of new objects,
 The transformation of known objects,
 The change of material for certain objects,
 The use of words combined with images,
 The putting to work of ideas offered by friends,
 The use of certain visions from half-sleep or dream."

Her Voice Over:
"To be with you I have to journey."

Her Voice Over:
"Wings of wind."

8. CROSS CUTS

INT.	LONDON HOTEL ROOM	NIGHT
INT.	BEDROOM	NIGHT

The operator speaks her name.
The English voice replies:
"Just a moment." Just a moment.
Just a moment. Time stops. Time flies.

Beyond his head the sun is dropping down,
The sky an orange, a green, a blue,
Light across the mountains and around his head.

She lifts the phone receiver.
The operator speaks her name.
She says hello.

Hello, hello.

Beyond her head the sky is dark and close,
Only the sinking moon, gibbous, nearly full,
The shadows of its mountains above her head.

Their voices ring with distance,
Echo with the journey into space,
The journey back, pass on the way, pass the moon,
Touch in relays, touch and tag.

"Do you remember me?" he says.
Her silence fills the space, the time,
This answer that words will not hold.

She sees the silver ring,
Ring that arrived in the mail,
Turns it on her finger, says his name.

I was losing your voice.
I can still make your voice ring on certain words.
I hold your voice to my ear, hold you.
We touch across the water, through the sky.
The moon moves from here to there,
From there to here.

They speak. They say goodbye.
Outside his window the sun disappears.
In the distant dark, she sees him walk outside
To see the moon's surprise.

Suddenly the air is so dry that it clicks.
His skin rasps against his clothes,
His eyes peel in their dry sockets,
His hands crackle as his fingers spread.

The hill drops away sharply underfoot,
Behind him the hollow shell of an unfinished house,
Before him the pale blue eastern sky
Where soon the white moon will rise
So soon after leaving her side.

He is walking in the woods,
Watching the day's slide,
Catching the light's moves,
Feeling the air suck him dry,
Skin and flesh and sinew and bone
And breath.

He catches his breath, leans against a tree,
Dry sapling, hears the light move
Around him, speaks her name three times,
Opens in to love, admits the day.

Voice Over:
"We shall sleep close as skin."

But his skin leaps, crisp and raw,
Snapping away from bone and bones,
Strips itself and leaps away,
Opens out to air and sky, skips
By the invisible moon, spreads
Thin as the membrane of an eye
Across the ocean to the east,
Leaps to her and leaves his bones
Staggered behind.

Voice Over:
"The mountain opens and admits you to light."

He wakes himself, the sunlight all around him
Plucking at his sleeves. He blinks
His dry eyes. He closes his hands hard
On skin and air.

There is moonlight in the room, no other light,
The moon itself not yet in sight, high overhead.
He is alone, lying back on the bed, muffled
In moonlight, lost in pale shadow, alone.

The past is moving in the dry dark around him,
Cold in his bones, his skin shivered and taut,
His eyes open and sightless, the whole room vague
As moonlight, as darkness, as a lunatic's eye.

He remembers:
The man whose voice he has never heard,
Whose name he only half knows,
The woman who starved herself to shadows,
Who begged his name for hours on end,
The man who turned and walked away,
His shoulders bent like stubs of wings,
The woman whose bones were hollow as a bird's,
Slim bones of a shrike or a bat,
The man who kept count on a yellow pad,
Who punched his scores deep like braille,
The woman who was sickened in her skin,
Who shook his arms in her own rage,
The man who called her name in the dusk,
Scratched at the ground and coughed fire,
The woman who called him on the phone
Until the phone bells broke and split,
The man who followed her from room to room,
Talking and holding the hurt in his side,
The woman whose tongue searched like a lizard,
Skittered and lurched from her lips,
The man who is waiting at the end of the world,
His mouth half open, his teeth gray and dull,
The woman who is waiting at the end of the world,
Her mouth half open, her teeth long and blunt.

These are demons. He knows that
Even as they linger in the faint air,
The familiar shapes of the familiar room,
Dresser and chair, the wide bed, the door,
Walls and windows and walls.

He looks to the window where the moon will soon appear.
There are clouds scratched across the silver sky.
He knows her pictures, photographs, are on the table there:
The one, she is dressed in black holding the black cat,
The other, white on white, and her face like a prayer.

He speaks her name, three times,
Feels the faith that works through love,
Knows the gift again, long his, long hers.

The future moves in the window like the moon,
Its shadowy mountains, its silent seas.
These people are not there. They are not here.

He remembers:
Her face in the rain, her open eyes,
How the past dissolves in water like a year,
How a stranger once lived inside his skin,
How only now he knows where he belongs.

The moon moves in the window like the future,
Its silent mountains, its luminescent seas.
He curves himself to sleep as though he were a spoon.
He dreams her there, cupped to him in this light,
Warm and close as skin as the moon moves by.

11. INT.   HIS DREAM   LATE NIGHT
    INT.   HER DREAM   EARLY MORNING

Moving toward the moon in the dark blue sky,
Dark blue clouds, the moon's clear eye,
They are flying over the ocean, flying east,
A rumble in this silence, in this dark blue dark,
A B-17, "Old Bill" from *Memphis Belle*,
Flying east to Egypt over the chopped waves,
The lines of ocean and the moon's reply,
Passing under the moon and an arrow of sky.

Night flight and celestial navigation,
Flying by the stars, letting light lead the way,
They are both dreaming and their dreams touch here,
High over water across the sky, this dark blue air,
Touch here and hold like hands, hold hard.

By night, they are departing to Egypt,
Flying to Egypt in this dark blue night,
To the dim Step Pyramid at Saqqara,
To Giza and Cheops' Great Pyramid,
And those of Mycerinus and Chephren,
To the secret Sphinx lit by electric light.

Voice Over:
"I have seen all of the suns men can remember."

The past opens the future, and they are flying
Past the moon in dark blue flight, flying
Past the ocean, past the sea, the river's slide,
To the sun and sun's opening eye, silver and enamel sun,
Enameled and silver eye, these two together
For this passing time, flying over water,
Over lone and level sands far away, closed eye and closed eye,
Eye to eye, together, asleep, dreaming the dream.

12. EXT.   ROAD   (FREEZING RAIN) NIGHT

Midnight and the moon lost in ice,
Black sky, black night,
And in the flickers of his flashlight
Only the glints and glazes of ice,
Slick black pavement, each blade of grass
Distinctly glassed, the iced tree limbs,
A fine mist of rain soothing down,
Ice and icing, who can stand before this ice?

A car has slanted across the steep road
Down to the frozen creek, the owner gone,
The car dark and empty, blocking the way,
So he is walking home, waving a beam
Of light before his careful shoes,
Choosing a way, the cold lighting his mind
Like a beacon in this coated dark.

It is only ice, an ice storm,
And he is walking home
In a moonless night, only that.

If she were here, he says,
Then it would be more than ice,
More than a night, this glimmer
Made real, this ice a continent,
This invisible night the moon's true abode.

He crosses the slippery bridge,
Skating each step beside the frozen rail,
Walks carefully along the curving road
And climbs the slow hill home.

Somewhere to the east, he says,
Vaguely up ahead, she stirs in her sleep,
Sees the world gleam like a mirror,
Sees through the glass into an icy night,
Sees this slick land, this single light,
Sees her face reflected silver like the sun,
Glass and mirror and ice, face to face,
And the one shining path that leads to home.

There is a way. She knows that.

She remembers the ways they found
To find each other, the spiral staircase
To a dining room, the mountain path,
The narrow walk where she took his arm,
Notes on the door, notes in the mail,
Bell's ring and the knock on the door,
The cold rain and the slick fast road,
The road to the airport and the road
Around town, driving through fog,
Walking through rain, running
In the clear cold dawn, a hand held out,
Another hand, hearts' directions
To the love that holds. There is a way.

She imagines a magic carpet
Sailing over a green sea, sea of hope,
Or a night flight to Egypt
As in a dream, imagines his face
Brushed by low clouds as by an angel's wing,
His hand holding hers, her sun's bright eye
Home in his sun's ring, imagines
A troupe of street musicians pausing
Just below her window to sing the song
They know so well, the three strong chords,
Imagines a breath in the room that chills
Her deeper than bone, that signs to her
That she is not alone, the gift
The gift beyond reward. There is a way.

She sees only the dull straight line
Of Montague Street, where Sherlock Holmes
First lived in London, lamp standards
And the passing cars, cold day, closed walls
Of the British Museum and the rows and rows
Of windows down the way. She sees no way.

But in the room behind her, all around her,
There are roses and the yellow scent of roses,
There is on her finger a silver ring

With its green stone, hope's green, love's green,
And the sun's eye sees what she does not see
But knows as she says his name three times,
Day's turn, world's window, the one sure way.

She remembers:

Dancers, dances, the lights' fall, light's burst,
How close they sit together, see together,
Write notes in silence, how the one dancer
Steps from light to shadow, how others move
From dark to light, the music, the applause,
How the shade of one dancer twists and turns
On the nearby wall, a shadow's dance so different
From the staid dance before them on the stage,
How for all the piping they do not dance,
How for all the wailing they do not weep.

They are at the dance concert, and when they leave,
Walking up the hill on the narrow walk,
She takes his arm with a hand that speaks
What neither of them knows to say,
These two friends suddenly shy,
Suddenly together, suddenly with something to say.

Voice Over:
"Unless you see signs and wonders you will not believe."

They sit for hours
To talk together, discuss weathers
And signs of weather, search for words
For ways of seeing, ways of saying,
They discuss forgotten lores, sign
And countersign, in a room rising with fish,
Fish on the walls, fish in the air,
Light moving like water, light even as air.

Voice Over:
"A thing which is present can be invisible,
Hidden by what it shows."

They are alone together in a room
And not alone, framed faces on the walls,
A darker shadow in a shadow, past
That lingers like a shadow, past

That opens like a window, hands
That balance a book together, rising sign
And ring of changes, change that rises,
Something here that is not present,
Something present that is not yet here.

Voice Over:
"To be with you I have to journey."

When he leaves, walking into weather,
She sees him as though he has just arrived,
She greets him in the doorway's shadow
With the one kiss she has to give,
The one gift he will return to give.

She knows that he is with her,
Knows that now they are together,
She notes and charts the changing weathers,
Changes and change, change and changes,
This motion like a fish through water,
This motion like an eye through air.

It all begins with a bird flying by
Backwards, trailing its cry behind
Like a string, the wind zagging
And dashing through sideways,
Light tossed crazyquilt on the ground
By the rails of the wrought-iron fence,
And cold air wrinkling over the grass
As though it were a desert day.

"This day is crazy," you hear a voice say,
"And it's all your fault." And it probably is,
If you could just figure out to whom
The judgment was addressed. Crazy day.
Sky clear as onions, inscrutable
As bananas while answering every question
Yes or no, X or Y, no or yes.

He is walking down the road,
Holding to the left side to face the traffic,
Breathing in the brightness of the day,
Reciting lines, trafficking in nonsense,
"We that are true lovers run into strange capers,"
And "A wise man's heart inclines him
Toward the right, but a fool's heart
Toward the left," and "Holla, you clown,"
Saying with every word to everyone
That he is a fool in the worst fool's way.

The day is tilted, sun on the left,
Tree on the right, right of way just ahead,
Dog in the ditch, cat at the wheel,
Electric lines looping out of sight,
Just like magic, sleight of hand,
Day palmed and made to disappear,
Reappears in jacket pocket, tangled
In a clump of keys like a heart.

You see the sun zip by, sky shade
To orange and green and red, night
Fall, stars wheel overhead,
Moon's late arrival. Dutch angles,

Low and high, wide angles, fisheye
Lens, too close, too far, too near.

He says, If she were here,
The day would waver and then balance,
Level as a head, even as an eye,
Find its own height like water,
Steady like light in the cold air.

He opens his hand, and the sky falls out,
Galaxies and hovering clouds, quasars
And spiralling nebulae, night like a face,
Her face, reflected in the sky.

He speaks her name and takes her hand
In his heart, a firm handshake,
Lapped thumbs and wrapped fingers,
And the landscape shouts, "Holla,"
And you hear applause like a ripe field
Of opening okra or a pasture
Filled with sleepy crows.

Holding a pen, writing a letter
On the pale blue paper of an aerogramme,
The only sound the heightened sound
Of the pen's point on the paper,
The quick starts and scratches,
The black loops and bends, turns and darts,
These thoughts, these words:

The sky is moving as though time were
Speeding up today (would that it were),
Dark gray clouds punctuating empty sky,
The day empty without you, the day
Filled with your presence in all ways.

I speak your name aloud and the room rings.

Read this letter as a hand, a palm
Where all the future lies, all these lines
And whorls, no lie, the truth revealed,
A landscape where you appear just there,
Just where the lifeline turns and soars away,
Or, read it as a hand that reaches
To your hand and holds it
Like a memory or a dream,
Holds it like a question or a prayer.

My hands across the water,
Our hands across this sky.

And I will read your letters once again,
The one essential scripture of my days
And nights, your script the writing
On the walls, writing on the moving air,
Writing on the moving world, wonder and sign.

And soon I'll sign my name and send
This on the way, folded and sealed,
Delivered up as evidence to those
Who care to see that, as the apostle says,
What we say by letter when absent,
We do when present, from hand to hand,

Hand in hand, at hand and far from hand,
Loved and loving, my love, to you, my love.

He signs his name.

They are sitting together around the fire,
And he is in the corner with his friends,
They are discussing books, two little books,
And when someone speaks her name, he looks
Aside, looks away, looks down, night and day,
He longs to see her, longs to be filled with joy.

One woman speaks of a day touched with grace,
The gift beyond reward; he speaks her name
As silent prayer, as thanks, as recognition.

Another woman speaks of a love so intense
That it brings with it attendant pain;
He speaks her name, pain flares like love.

A man speaks of the spirit's climb from church
To God, the door that opens, window's width,
Height of an eye; he says her name as sign.

The wood snaps and spirals into smoke
Behind, beyond these men, these women,
This weighing of words, word touching word,
Word's way and word's echo, word on word,
The fire's light winking and withdrawing,
The room's ring closing like a spoken word.

He leaves the room by gift of mind and eye,
Swirls like smoke and disappears, wavers
Like rain and spreads across the sky,
Finds her in distant London curled in sleep,
Touches her like a breeze, like a question,
Fits to her body like a spoon a spoon,
Speaks to her in her dream, my love, my love.

And never leaves the room, hears every word,
Speaks aloud his daily prayer, prayer of the flesh,
Prayer of the heart, "I'm sorry, and thank you,
Thank you," adds silently, thank you, thank you,
Grace and love and spirit's climb, smoke
Like a dream, sky like smoke, night like a winter sky
With the stars like beacons pointing out the way.

18. INT.   CAR   (RAIN) NIGHT

They remember:

First Sunday in Advent, the new year
Begins, and they are in his car, together
In his parked car, lit by a streetlight,
Listening to the surge and ebb of rain,
Rain glowing down the windshield,
Rain shined and glancing on the hood,
Rain to dissolve the past, night
Turned and turning, talking in the rain.

Voice Over:
"The night is far advanced; the day is at hand."

They are wrapped in heavy coats,
Breath fogging the cold wet air,
Face to face at last, alone, together,
Speaking in the rising rain, watching
A stranger stride across the shining grass,
Walk by, hearing the rain's rhythm
And each other, talking together,
Listening to each other, alone.

The past rocks the car like a demon,
Their hearts locked and skipping,
The night like a vise pressing in,
Worries like the breath of demons,
Their teeth cracking on the car roof
Like rain, their leathery wings
Smacking at the ground and dragging
Across the wide wet glass.

Voice Over:
"No one who waits for you shall be put to shame."

He watches her face with the care of a scholar,
He studies the way her head turns, movement
Of a hand, eyes turning as she watches the rain
Slip light across the glass, watches light's shadow
Flow across his face, across his hands,

Light's shadow like a wing, brushed pinions
Of an angel's wing, breath like water or fire,
The angel that bears the gift beyond reward
That day and hour, grace unquestioned,
Grace unquestionable, wings that move
Like the moving rain, rise and fall,
The shifting syllables of this night's rain.

Voice Over:
"Now is the time for us to rise from sleep."

If Bergman were directing this scene,
His blue watch cap pulled snug against the rain,
His viewing lens in hand, you would hear
No voices, only now the violoncello
Of Käbi Laretei, resonant and rich
As rain, and the light's single flare
Like a cupped yellow rose.

You do hear only the heightened background
Of the rain, see only those faces
Silhouetted in this car, see
This conversation, hear this rain,
Know the angel's passage
And the demons' rattling fear.

Voice Over:
"Now is the time for us to rise from sleep."

Before this night is over, that day and hour
Arrived, daybreak, sun's tiger stalk
And her waking jumbled thought: *the soul
Of the tiger is talk*, before the day's arrival,
He will ask her in this rain and darkness
To marry him, and she will answer
In this rain, this curling light.

He takes her hand, and they are silent.
The rain speaks to darkness, speaks
In light, light that is so bright
It nearly blinds the eye that sees,
Rain so steady, so insistent
It nearly drowns the ear that hears.

[36]

It is the first Sunday in Advent,
Beginning of the holy year.
There is an angel moving in this darkness.
There is a light shining
In this talk you do not hear.

Ice again, this time a dust of snow,
A pale powder and then the rain,
An ice clean and shining, each twig,
Each blade of grass encased, inclining,
Trees and power lines snapping like fingers,
The day reminding him of other days,
How the past dissolves in water like a year,
How rain and freezing rain convoy
His thoughts across the world,
Making it new, slicking it in ice,
Making it shine like the dream child
Of the silver sun it is.

He is walking through the ice and rain,
Walking the miles to the mailbox and back,
Carrying her a letter that others must bear
Across the water, through the sky.

He recites to himself, keeping warm,
Words from another letter, a letter
That arrived this day, an Easter letter
In this land of snow and ice, time
Spinning ahead like a car on ice,
My every desire fulfilled in love alone,
He says, repeats and says again as sign,
My every desire, he says, every desire
Fulfilled in love alone, in love alone.

The ground sings under his boots,
A crackle and slide, song of the ice,
Hoarfrost of heaven, harmony
Of water and freezing air. The gray sky
Dims as he goes, sun's secret descent,
Mountains' rise, day's going into night.

He makes his way, makes a way, makes way,
Across this icy day, this coming night,
In haste, in joyous hurry, in love alone.

In this dark, lit only by firelight
In a cold dark house, this wave and waver
Of blue and yellow flame, he hears
Ice moving in the night, ice crack
And crash, ice splitting trees
And drawing them down to earth,
The whole city dark and cold, caught
And still like a fish in sudden ice,
Ice and sirens' whoops and trembles,
Electrical pops and slaps that break
The sky with quick green light,
Ice moving in, ice come to stay.

He is alone and lonely, allowing
Light from his flashlight beam
To show each tree a shining cluster,
Lighting light and light and light
And light, a galaxy of tree, tree
And dying tree, tree caught and held,
The ice shattering underfoot
Should he venture out like glass
In his throat, glass on his tongue,
This night sky flashing like a sign
From heaven, dark woe and cold comfort,
Like a sign, ice come to stay.

Caught like a fish, he says, caught
And frozen like a fish. He says
Her name a single frozen time,
This man in love alone, then says her name
And sees the gold flicker of flame
Along the wood's bright rim,
Like a fish, he says, and tugs
Absently his silver chain, the sun,
As he watches the flame's dart
And flash, hears its splash
And sigh, says her name again
And feels his heart jump like a fish.

In this cold dark house:
In this motion:
This prayer:

For my sorrow in this depth of joy,
Gift beyond reward, I'm sorry.
For the joy I feel in this broken world,
This sorrow, this woe, I thank you,
I thank you.

Prayer of the given world,
Prayer of the frozen grass,
Sheathed blade and blade and blade,
Prayer of the shattered tree,
Prayer of the rabbit in the road,
Prayer of the white crowned sparrow
Pitched stiff by the feeder, iced,
Prayer of the weed and creeping vine,
Prayer of the bent tree, twisted
And leaning, leaning and turned,
Prayer of the saw blade,
Prayer of the chisel,
Prayer of the roadsign, iced over
And glaring,
Prayer of the hand,
Prayer of the thigh,
Prayer of the eye, open and trying to see,
Prayer of the mind, confused
And thanks giving,
Prayer of the ice,
Prayer of the moving air,
Prayer of the sun, invisible
And clouded from rising to setting,
Prayer of the earth,
Prayer of the world, this motion,
This turning,
Prayer of the lover, this prayer,
Lover and lover, distant and loving,
Alone and lonely, alone in love
Fulfilled, prayer and prayers,
This prayer of thank you,
This motion of thanks,
This dark cold house of thanks.

22. INT./EXT.   HIS DREAM/THE OPEN WINDOW   NIGHT/NIGHT

He remembers:

A hot damp night in December,
Windows open and a madness mixed in the warm south wind,
Dark figures moving in this warm air,
The night moving like madness and slow desire.

He is asleep.
This dream arrives:

He feels them pass him by,
Their stale dry breath, their arms
Dangled and flapping like empty sleeves,
Feels them pass him by,
His blood shrunk in his veins,
His spine shivering like a struck dog's tail,
Feels them pass him by,
Blind and driven, blind and driving by,
They move like dirty curtains,
The dust unsettled behind their silent feet,
He feels them pass him by.

Time drains and pools,
A silence as in heaven, as in hell,
Time stagnant and slow and warm,
Time clotting, cold and congealed.

He sees her there, just ahead,
She is lying on her back, her arms limp,
Her eyes empty, her head thrown back,
Her neck open like a sore,
The red blood welling out and spilling
To the splintered floor,
And they are poised over her like sculpture,
Like something caught and pinned
In a passing headlight, something dark
And brushed backwards, bristling and hackled,
The woman's sharp face like a broken shark's tooth,
Edged and ragged,
The man's smooth face, blank and vacant
Like a quick erasure,
Their mouths slick with spittle and blood,
Their eyes pressed back into their heads

Like cornered bats, sick and crawling,
Blood peeling back their narrow lips,
Their stained teeth like broken bottles,
Their hands like leaking faucets,
Four sharp eyes glazed and glaring
As her blood tints their tongues
And slides down the yearning tubes
Of their hollow throats, yanking in their necks
Like coupled snakes, their dry hearts
Stretched to the damp like the brittle corpses of worms.

He awakens to the heat,
The window sighing the curtains in,
So cold that he shakes with the chill,
Huddles deep into himself,
Tries to dispel the demons of this dream
By simple force of will,
By saying aloud the new facts of the morning,
Sunlight on the sill, clock's face,
The number of the day, but he cannot
Say her name.

He no longer remembers:

The passage of the day, his deeds,
The work he did, the thoughts he had.

He does remember:

Sitting in an open window
Late the next night, half inside,
Half out, the warm night stirring
As in a dream.

He tells her the dream,
And his voice ices and seals over.

He reaches to her hand,
And she holds his like an answer
Or a promise.

She leaves the room, returns to bring him
A silver and enamel sun,

A ring, an amulet or talisman, a sign
Swung on a silver chain around his neck.

It moves as he remembers:

How more signs would follow, how cold air
Punched in the night, how winter staked
Those windows shut, how lights began
To move and beckon in the darkness,
How hands held together like promises
Or like answers.

He remembers:

How two demons blew and scattered in the air
Like dust or like dry echoes, how they disappeared
Like mildew in the new sun's dawning,
How the night air cleared like a cured eye,
And rain followed as the past dissolved,
How he learned the lessons of faith,
The lessons of learning, how he spoke
Her name and she answered, how
Time shifts like fog on a winter road,
How he knows her name like the one right answer,
How the gift beyond reward
Hangs round his neck like tomorrow,
How every desire is fulfilled
In love alone.

Her hands:
This motion:
This grace:
Her hands held out to the light,
Her hands turning in the light,
Her hands holding yellow roses
Or cupping yellow roses in the air,
Her hands pressing the pen onto the page,
Drawing an untethered balloon, taut lines
And wickerwork gondola, set to sail
Across wide water, or setting down words
For him to read and memorize,
She spreads her hands, links thumbs,
And they are wobbling butterflies
Or an angel's graceful wings,
A prayer of angles,
Prayer of fingers, prayer of hands,
She lets them droop,
Then lifts them out like clouds
Or opening windows,
She folds and pops up finger and finger
To make a demon's horns,
They disappear into an open hand,
A wave, no tricks, just like the goofy wave,
Thumb in ear, she gave him when they first met,
Her hands holding each other,
One hand (the right) touching
The slim silver ring, green stone,
She wears on the other,
Her hands opening and closing
To iris in and out the scene across the way,
Her hands are small,
She worries that her hands are thick,
That light will shine through her sister's hands,
Not hers, and as she raises her hands,
Opens them to show just what she means,
They glow like light itself.

He counts them over,
These letters from a distant lover,
Her letters, cards and letters,
Blue and white and colored paper,
He shuffles, stacks and cuts them
Like a deck of worn familiar cards,
Face cards (her face), queen of hearts,
King and jack, clubs and spades
And red diamonds, day on day on day:

The Magritte card, wings like prayers,
Sky through sky and waving water,
The card of London tilted
From the air, card of London
Close-up on the ground, card
Like a heart, the queen and Philip
Standing proud, "Love from LONDON,"
And the letters, blue air letters,
The first fat letter, jet lagged
And filled with desperation,
The ones *par avion* (by George),
The white one from the Tate
With its address in hopeful ink
(Green, green and red),
The long rectangle of pink and blue,
The blue air letter with the drawn balloon,
Her figure in the basket, her waving hand
Across the water on the back,
The letters from the ballet (*Manon*)
With the dancers moving like dreams,
About the play (*As You Like It*)
With its foolish words and words
Of love, the one about the Turners
In the Tate, "light as surprising
As blindness," hello and hello,
Love's language in distance and time,
The card with the fool and the tree,
The card with the sunrise and sea
(Turner's, of course), the card
With "two opalised gastropods,"
Shells for sign of pilgrimage,

These pilgrim's letters, pilgrim's songs,
These words from afar,
These hands held close across water,
Across distance, across time,
This necessary scripture
That he studies with an eye
Made sharp and fine by love alone.

25. INT.   THEATER   NIGHT

She remembers:

A tale of love and loss, exile and death,
Manon, the seat, how she shifts back and forth
To try to see the dancers moving like a dream
Beyond the thick round head in front of her,
These dancers moving like shadows on a wall,
So substantial, muscle and muscle, back and thigh,
Turning to music like planets to a distant star.

She feels her own sun's eye move on its silver chain,
She touches the chain along her throat,
She moves in music like a dance,
She flies away, she flies across the silent water.

I never knew, she thinks, that I could ever be
Alone like this. I never knew, she thinks,
That I could ever be so far from what I know
As this. I never knew, she thinks, how love alone
Can matter in a world so full of things.

"When I was at home," she recites softly to herself,
"I was in a better place, but travelers
Must be content." Shakespeare. *As You Like It.*
She thinks of love, recites another line,
"My affection hath an unknown bottom
Like the Bay of Portugal." Also *As You Like It.*
She thinks of other plays she's seen,
Antony and Cleopatra, desperate love,
Caught time, "I am dying, Egypt, dying,"
And she thinks of Egypt, Egypt before her,
Dream like a promise, Egypt in white moonlight,
Egypt in his hand, in the familiar curve of his face,
Egypt as familiar as the mountains of the moon.

The music absorbs her, fills her like water,
Splashes around her like fresh air,
She holds the tiny silver eye in her hand
As though it were the world, as though it were
His hand. When I was home, she thinks.

Home, she thinks. Egypt, she thinks.
So far away, she thinks and bows her head.

The music stops and leaves a silence
For a moment, a stillness in this motion,
A pause in air like a leaping fish,
And then applause washes over her like rain,
Dissolves distance and her thoughts,
These clashing palms, these shouts,
This loud applause, as the air fills
With roses arcing toward the stage,
The air around her thick with roses,
Yellow roses that fill her eyes like tears,
Roses that move the air to music like a dance.

A day of fragments,
Opalescent, light and light,
A flash in bone and nerve,
Star burst and eye's surprise:

He sits in the dark room,
Only one dim light, he sorts
These fragments with a jeweler's care,
Sorts them out and stores them all away:

The wind's high hustle at the window,
The sharp clear sky, the clown's red nose
He wears around the house, fool's nose,
Sign of the wisdom of the heart,
And the new crystal heart, a gift from her,
Almost as heavy as his own fool's heart,
Her voice again on the telephone,
With greetings across water, questions,
Plans, the sound of her voice in tears,
Sound that splits his heavy heart
Like crystal or like a gem,
New letters in the mail, voice from a week ago,
Voice from two days ago, songs on the radio,
You send me, send me, my life,
Sultans of swing, words from St. Augustine,
The past does not exist, words
From a letter (hers), the past is dead,
The words they say to each other,
My life, send me, sultans of swing,
We need not say anything, red nose
Like a clown, Bozo or Christ the Clown,
Her voice crackling out through space
And down, a cry and crying, a true hello,
Hello, his name, her name, crystal heart,
The words they do not need to say but do,
Day shaken as they are shaken, so far away,
So far apart, piece it together and find
Only the words they need not say,
Love and love, her name (three times),
His name, heart like a stone, hearts
As clear as crystal, day like a clown,

Day like a song, day that is past,
Day that lives in memory like a gem,
Day like an opal, day like a lucky star.

She is sitting in a room, a room
Of black and white, lines and planes,
Edges and lines, planes that do not fly,
Sitting by the silent telephone,
Recalling his voice on the line,
So far away, his laugh, her name, so far
She wants to fly away, fly across
This night, through the ice that mars
The inside of the windowpane
Like the pebbled back of a crystal heart,
Fly over lonely water, fly by moonlight
Or the dark of the moon, fly to Egypt
By flying the other way, flying home.

She does not know where she goes next,
To bitter Germany perhaps, sharp
And unreal as the past, to Heidelberg,
Or perhaps not, only knows that she will not go,
Not soon, to where she wants to be.

The night knocks at the glass,
She will not let it in, not now.

She wears the gifts he sent her,
No roses, now abandoned, now blown
And gone, but she wears the chain
Just by the eye, the tiny golden heart
They found once on the floor, lost
Then finally found again, she wears
The pin with its two clasped hands,
Hands across the water, hands holding
With identical blue sleeves,
And, of course, the ring, the silver ring
With its stone of green, this vow,
This promise from the past,
This continuing present from the past,
This emblem of a future now begun.

I must glitter, she says, like an opal
In sunshine, like a prism in a window,
And her eyes swell with water, catch light
Like an opal or an icy window in the dawn.

She thinks of the photographs she's taken,
Of the things she's seen through that round lens,
Light disguised as a wall, light disguised
As a window, shadow passing as light,
Light alone, shadow passed.

The night knocks, she snaps
The light and lets it in.

In a black and white room, she dreams
In color, hugs herself to herself,
Sees him just now, six hours ago,
And he is dancing, dancing to himself,
Dancing under a paper lamp,
Dancing in a clown's red nose,
The music turned up loud,
Dancing all around the room,
Girded in gladness, her gifts,
Wearing his thick warm socks,
The blue shirt grinning like the moon,
Carrying the heart she gave him
In a pocket by his heart, or in his hand,
He is dancing, she says,
Dancing alone all around the room,
Dancing me home.

He remembers:

A month and a day ago,
Two days after Christmas,
The sun gone and no moon at all,
A black sharp night, the stars
Wheeling up and over their heads,
A passage of light and light and light,
Uncountable light, and the darkness dizzy
With the dance, this chill step across the sky.

Voice Over:
"The only knowledge is love."

They visit the observatory,
Bundled up in the small dome,
Holding tight, the sky reeling
And their breath dancing on their lips
In small reflection. They watch
The dome pivot and follow the sky,
The slim telescope balanced on itself
Like a delicate dream, catching the light
And the light beyond the light,
Line and depth and distance, star
And star, space, cloud and dust,
Distance and presence and absence,
This galaxy, this universe, this home.

Voice Over:
"The only knowledge is love."

They see the Pleiades and the invisible pyramid
Of stars beyond the Pleiades, made visible,
Made clear to these who have eyes to see,
And the Great Nebula of Orion, rising,
Curling like a whiff of smoke
Or a coil of breath in the chill night air,
And hanging low over the nearby hills,
Colored in shimmering earth light
Red, blue and white, Jupiter and four moons,

Low and trembling, tinted by light's illusion,
By light's mutable surprise. She takes his arm,
And then he holds her to him, close together
Under a sky glowing like an angel's wing,
While the dome rumbles and swings around
And the sky revolves and sheds its light.

Voice Over:
"The only knowledge is love."

How they have managed to find each other
Neither knows, or if he imagines he knows,
He does not know as he ought to know,
These two friends, this love in the turning light,
Mystery beyond mystery, gift beyond reward,
These two lovers close as a double star,
Circling each other, ring and ring,
Voyaging to Arcturus and farther, to stars
And stars, to spiralling space, opening out
And opening in, cosmos curving like a wing,
Infinities clasping hands through this dark sky.

Voice Over:
"The only knowledge is love."

She says the word *love*, says the word
World, says the word *grace*, and he hears
Her faith opening the night
As it fills the day, light beyond light.

He hears the word *love*, hears the word
World, hears the word *grace*, the voice
That speaks in every voice, the greeting
(Hello, hello) that shines in this dark sky,
That speaks from planets lit by the absent sun,
That speaks in his hand holding her shoulder,
Or echoes in the astronomer's quiet delight.

Voice Over:
"The only knowledge is love."

The dome slaps shut, and they descend the stair,
A tight spiral to the floor below, they sign

The book, "Sky leaps as earth sleeps,"
They walk out together on the dark flat earth,
Knowing that soon she will fly up and make it round,
Fly up and fly away. Jupiter is a white blur,
And the Pleiades are tiny and far, the Great Nebula
Not even there. They hold to what they do not see.
They know what they see and what they hold.
He takes her hand and knows for now
What he ought to know.

Voice Over:
"The only knowledge is love."

29. INT./EXT.   AIRPORT   DAY

He remembers:

The suspended day, sky white
As a stone, heart like a stone,
She is going away, so far away,
The tails of the airplanes
Outside the high glass window
Like chimney pots outside another window,
A window on a rainy day,
Rain washing down, the suspended prisms
In the window catching only rain,
Sending only rain's echo around the room.

He sees her there alone, she will walk
Through the empty house, will find
A picture on the wall she has not seen,
His picture, picture from the past,
A stranger's face, as she recalls
The face she knows, his face, her love
So far away.

Voice Over:
"The past dissolves in water like a year."

She is with him now, alone together, waiting
In a room full of friends, of family, of strangers,
Touching and standing apart, lost
And together, found and apart,
The flat white sky outside the window
Like a stone with a new name written on it,
A small stone in his palm or slipped into his pocket,
A name which no one knows.

Voice Over:
"To be with you I have to journey."

They kiss at the barricade,
The one kiss they have to give,
Love given, love received, gift beyond reward,
And she walks away without looking back.

The day stands still.

He stands beside the chainlink fence
And sees her climb into the waiting plane.
She does not see him there. She knows him there.
He holds his hand against the chainlink fence.
The day is like a white stone,
The blue tails of the airplanes
Like crosses or letters, hieroglyphs
Against a stone white sky.

Voice Over:
"The only knowledge is love."

The airplane blusters and shakes
The frozen air, the solid ground,
This moment like a stone. It taxis off.
It rolls along and rolls aloft.
It disappears into the empty sky,
And it is gone.

The sky is white and bent
Like an angel's wing. There
Are no shadows anywhere.
The sky is white and smooth
Like a smooth white stone.
He says her name once,
Then two more times. He sees
The new name written on the stone,
The white stone of the sky,
Stone he holds in his hand.
He receives the name and knows it.
It is now his own.

The sun moves windy shadows across his face,
The splashing shadows of blown leaves,
Branches and leaves, they dance like fish
In a sunny bowl, light and shadows,
The sky washed clean and pale blue
As though by light itself, light
Of the sightless sun, light of the moon,
New moon, dark sphere and curved light,
A crinkle of mountains all along the arc,
The moon that swung slow across the sky
Last night, moon that she may be watching
Now, somewhere to the north, somewhere
To the east, somewhere on this small world,
Small blue world, shadowed with clouds,
Turning with its turning moon
Through the turning time of space,
This turning space of time.

He is holding a card, "Lover attains
The Rose," from the *Roman de la Rose*
(Actual size), the lover looking like a fool
With his long gray staff, his odd red hat,
The garden fenced and walled, the rose
Flatly drawn and red, but on the back,
Stitched with red thread just beside his name,
Name written on the card as on white stone,
Name written in her hand, a yellow rose,
A yellow rose, Lover attains the Rose.

The light wrinkles the card in his hand,
The rose moving for a moment like a dream,
Dream of Egypt, darkening for a moment
As though a demon's dusty wing had crossed it,
Cast it into sudden eclipse, then passed away.

He thinks of Guillaume de Lorris and Jean de Meun,
Those who set forth verses in writing, *Roman de la Rose*,
His own words, hers, these two friends, two lovers,
Who say as they see, who say thanksgiving
For everything they see with each word they say,
Love, world, grace, thank you, thank you,
Lover attains the Rose, attains the Rose.

The sun moves on by, light through the window
Moving as it moves, the wind's reply,
This dance of light upon his hands,
Upon his face, this gift beyond reward,
This love, this world, this grace,
This joy that moves through darkness,
Moves through light, each day new as the moon,
Renewed and borne anew by light itself.

They imagine:
This motion:
These motions:
This grace:

The airport with its roof curved like a wing,
An angel's wing, he says, lifted for flight,
Awaiting her return, for here she will return,
Here she will circle and turn and alight,
This airport they remember, this airport
They imagine, this day not in darkness,
Day that will not surprise them like a thief
In the night, gift beyond reward, this light.

Her return:
He imagines:

First, her face across the way, through glass,
A barricade of customs men, who glare,
Who wave him away, her hand raised in surrender
Or in distant greeting, her hand held high,

Or, her face pale and drawn, ill,
Her eyes like dark pools in her pale face,
Pools unstirred, the water deep and still,
Frail, her face lined and drawn, so ill,

Or, they are running in slow motion
As in certain movies they both know,
Run toward each other forever, nearing
And never touching, as in her dream,
When they passed like wind in the night
And never met, never met,

Or, most often, her face open like a dream,
Smiling the way he has seen it before,
Her hands shedding light, open to light,
Silver ring and silver chain, sun's eye
Open and waiting for its aureole, its ring,
Her voice speaking his name, gift beyond reward.

Her return:
She imagines:

First, encumbered and caught in customs,
Her cases crammed and three bags full
Of things she could not bear to leave behind,
Letters from a distant land, or dreams,

Or, his face, unfamiliar, young and strange,
A face she has seen on a wall, in a picture,
In a photograph, a stranger's face, face
That will not know her, will look right past,

Or, they are running in slow motion
As in certain movies they both know,
Run toward each other forever, nearing
And never touching, as in her dream,
When they passed like wind in the night
And never met, never touched, never met,

Or, most often, he is there as familiar
As her own hand, his face a greeting
She has seen before, a paper yellow rose
Pinned to his lapel, hands open, arms,
Heart, a glint of silver by his throat,
Sun's blind eye eager to receive its sight again.

Voice Over:
"Light that opens the day of open windows."

Voice Over:
"No one who waits for you shall be put to shame."

Voice Over:
"Now is the time for us to rise from sleep."

Her return:
They imagine:

They are at the airport. They are together,
The journey past, the distance dissolved
In presence like a dream, the past resolved
In hand and hand and hand and hand.

[61]

They are at the airport. They are still apart,
Watching each other through glass, across
A barricade, eye's water catching light
Sudden as a fish, sudden as explosive laughter,
Sudden as two hands' quick break into applause.

They are at the airport, swimming in winter light,
Diving and splashing in a late slant of winter light,
Day after day opening like windows to the light,
These children of the light, these walkers on light,
These two friends, these two lovers, this light.

They are at the airport, alone with strangers,
Together with a multitude of friends, giving
The gift they have been given to all they meet,
Thank you, thank you, gift beyond reward,
Gift beyond thanks, gift that must be seen to be seen.

Voice Over:
"The only knowledge is love."

These events will occur:

The airport building, like a pyramid
Or vast forgotten Egyptian tomb, opened up
By love to light, will stir and lift
Like a wing, an angel's wing, she says,
Its shadow like a drift of light,
Like light itself.

He will be wearing a paper yellow rose,
Handmade and foolish in his left lapel,
A clown's mad grin on his face,
His eyes slick with water, slick with light.

She will be wearing a silver ring
On the likeliest finger of her left hand,
A pin with two hands clasping across water
On her coat, her eyes alert with light.

They will hold each other close for hours,
For days, the sun slipping over and out,
Over and out, over and out, nights
Winking by with scarcely even a nudge.

They will never part, he says, she knows,
They both believe, these two so far apart,
So far away, so close and now together,
So close that they can never part again.

You see them standing close together,
Hand in hand, or hand on arm,
Or held in silence in love's embrace,
These two familiar faces, two friends,
Two lovers, two voyagers in space,
This space of time, these two you know so well.

Their hands open into fingers, palms
And fingers, and they wave right at you
From the screen, they say, "Hello, hello."
The light beam that wavers just above
Your head holds them there like a dream,
Or a promise, or the answer to a question
You almost have forgotten how to ask.

They hold each other and they wave hello.

Light fills the air as from an open window.

Light fills your eyes like tears.

These hands, held open, wave a fond hello.

Voice Over:
"Receive your sight; your faith has made you well."

THE END

from *THE DAY I STOPPED DREAMING ABOUT*
  BARBARA STEELE

Here we are all, by day; By night w'are hurl'd
By dreames, each one, into a sev'rall world.

— Robert Herrick

THE DAY I STOPPED DREAMING ABOUT
BARBARA STEELE

The drizzle shifted,
A bird drowsy with rain
Yawned into song,
The foghorn ran down.

Below the castle walls
Her head grisly with masks
The long slices of her sides
And the heavy dog's howl
(I hear the clamor of horses
  And the long rope to which I am attached
  Buckles beneath me)
The knotted arm
And the long sinew
That lays itself along
The long curve of her side.

Blond, her legs curved
To the horse's flank,
Making the sun dance
To the blue of her eyes

(Is the last dream before waking
  More flesh than real,
  More real than the dark before?)

The horse dances
And she is as purely naked
As the pine-needled dawn
And the dogs run lazy and smooth
In the tall grass.

The bronze door,
Stone,
A muffled cry,
The iron maiden,
And the sun
Crazy with its own size
In the moving lake
Where her horse lowers its head to drink
And she sleeps on his arching spine.

ANOTHER RIDE WITH GOAT McGUIRE

for Louis D. Rubin, Jr.

Old Goat McGuire, his whisky breath,
Remembers, lifts his head to laugh,
Two crummies and a load of dynamite,
The snow that night, the northern pines
All black and white, the burning wood,
Steam up, the bell, the engine and
Those turning wheels, snow blew, and Goat,
Old Goat McGuire came through.

Long ago that ride. Too long now.
No cars rattle on that logging track,
The woods all stumped and gullied out,
And Goat more wrinkled than he was before.
The barn door bangs, car barn, round
House, the engines gone, not even rust
Remains.

       Perhaps a handcar sits hidden
In the dust, dark in a shadow, no corner
For the house is round; but then no car,
No wheels at all, and Goat, old Goat,
His whisky breath, looks all around
And leaves.

       No work here and now,
His bottle empty (it clatters and then
Shatters in the cluttered tracks,
In the dry and weedy dark), Goat
Turns onto the open road, weaves down
The track, no red light (or green),
No arms salute his smoking breath,
The track is clear.

      And back in town
The diesels pass, the long cars tiered
With automobiles, the boxcars and the angry
Horns. No, that's no world for Goat
McGuire, hero of a snowy night, two
Crummies and a load of dynamite. Old

Goat, he wanders down the track, turns
Off and down the bank, heads home, his
Whisky breath, his sagging bed, so warm,
His old and sleeping wife. Street lights
Glow green, three trees that hold their leaves
And keep them green despite the night,
The coming cold. He whistles, long and low,
Claps down his arms, and Goat, Old Goat McGuire
Goes home.

INSIDE SALLY

First off, there were the fans,
Flashes of pure blond, blue
Lights and Clair de Lune

The crouching quarterback

The fans, that taut balloon,
And movement, movement
On the stage, the lights,
The frozen room, the fans

A roaring in the circling stands,
The crouching quarterback,
A Princeton boy, arms striped

"I never quite understood it,
This sex symbol," said Marilyn
Monroe before she died. They named
A life preserver for Mae West.
Jean Harlow, her platinum hair, died
Of her kidney, and Brigitte Bardot,
At thirty years, is still troubled
By acne.

There was, of course, music,
Au Clair de Lune, and fans,
A thousand fans, blond rhythm
In those curling wings

The crouching quarterback,
A Princeton boy, striped arms,
Calls Inside Sally, his wingback
Takes the ball, a play as naked
As the moon,

   and understands.

AN OPT FOR THE CARPENTER

for Julia Randall

We are staid puritans, and we are creative
carpenters, and we are in between, and the
world's future depends on our choice.
I opt for the Carpenter.

The puritan carpenter, all nails
And heavy hammer, dark, tall
Hat, brim wide and black, stark
And angled in the snow. No

Walrus here, no singing shells,
And dancing teardrops in the sand.

Plain song, and the words: hard
Wood and harder iron, the cross.

He builds a cross — bare, naked,
Sharp against the pines and snow,
Blunt against the sun gone gray.
A heavy cross that bends his back
And bends his brow.

           How did we
Get here? What seas did we cross?
What have we done to hang here
While his hollow eyes stare up?

No.

     No puritan carpenter like this.
Let's embellish a bit. Toss in a bird,
Flowers, maybe even children who laugh
In all that gray. Too much? But
There they are: birds, children,
Laughers and scratchers, the heel
And toe, the in and out, the dance.

Set a grin on the carpenter's teeth,
Grit as he will. And let's see,

Perhaps a maypole in the forest
Made in a familiar style, bare now,
Naked, sharp against the pines and
Snow, anything (or maybe everything)
But blunt. Perhaps a slyness in his eye,
A gleam, a touch of scarlet somewhere
In his mind. Gaunt but gay. Too much?

It is possible, or so I am told, to twist
Nails, sharpen both their ends, link them
To chains, tie them for beds. Puritan?
Perhaps. Let's opt for the carpenter
Who drives them clean, creates his forms
For us to decorate. Let's opt for art
And spread color on his frame, red,
Green for spirit, gold, yellow, on
And on. Of black let's whiten
White, and paint that cross, for it
Is bare: no one hangs there. Long
Gone and left us room to move.

No. No walrus here, none needed,
Nor empty shells, for them no need, no
Room. There's people here, and words,
All colors, sizes, shapes confound
The eye, the ear. Come all this way?
For this? Look down. Look up.
The carpenter is at his work.
The sun slits ribbons in the darkened wood.

WHY WERE THE BANDIT'S EYES
HIDDEN BEHIND A GREEN MASK?

The stuttering bishop,
The midwife,
And there were the children
Strung across the highway
Like Christmas festoons.

The carriage was of gold
And gleamed,
And the peasants bore rakes
To ravish the ladies.
(That year was a time.)
The leaves fell early.

The dust lay low.

The horse's ears were back,
His beribboned tail,
The pinwheels of his eyes,
The foam,
His teeth were flat and wide,
And the bridge we never reached.

THE BLACK FINGER

How slyly it moves
Into layers of cloth
To pop the buttons off.

The bed was hung in silk
And soft. Her head,
The golden hair around
It spread. Her limbs,
Composed. Her eyes,
Closed.

The wreaths, the bawdy
Beaux, the iron bells.

The pigeons dive into the wind
To spin Saint Catherine's wheel.
And sip, sip, sip, a pink,
Lace frosted glass, a wink.

The feet whisper,
Crepe rustles,
Whisper, whisper,
The windows are closed.

The fat man sops his brow.
So primly propped.

TANJONG MALIM: 1934

Rain on the roof, bamboo,
His hand, the glass, splintered
Fingernails and wrinkled suit,
Dirty white, his face, the suit,
And chuk, chuk, chuk, the wooden
Paddles of the turning fan.

Malays, empty faces, rubber pots,
The rows and rows of draining trees,

And now the rain, the heat, his face
Is dry, his eyes are blank, but not

Within

      a dancer, small child, girl,
Her hands are sinuous as her eyes,
Thin thighs, small feet, the ching,
And ching, ching, ching, musicians
Drunk with god and wine, it sways,
Her head, the hollow clong and ching,
Ching.

Mildewed piano, broken keys, old songs,
Moons, loves that last, broken hearts,

(Outside in the rain, sleek with rain,
Eyes slit toward the light, the sound,
The curve of his knife easy on his finger's
Tip, he crouches, watches, waits, waits.)

Pasteboard lovers, counterfeit love, and baby
Wait for me, for me, old tinkle, clatter
And the negro's hands, his teeth gone,
Sings with tight lips, old songs,

              the clong,
And clatter, so small, in his hands so small,
A child,

              our love,
A moon, Miami in the spring, Paree, Dubuque,

she moved like silk, was dirty,
Small, ching, ching, no sobs, just silk,
The clong, clatter, cries, and ching.

His hand lies easy on the drink, he doesn't
Drink, his face is dirty white and gray,
And listens to the rain, the rap and tattle
Of the rain, no songs, just rain, and whispers
In the bar, (The dark is wet and waits.) his
Eyes are open, chuk, chuk, chuk and chuk, the rain,
The rain upon the bamboo shutters and the roof.

A hollow clong, cluk, ching and ching.

DESERT FOX

for C. W. Parker

The general knows. His maps
Spread on the table, creases
And all. And his pointer ceases
To make sense, just waggles up
And down. But he knows.

The grumble of the idling
Tanks below the window.
Their guns are muffled
Canvas in the dust.

"Must we always assault
From the rear, when most
Often a frontal thrust
Meets with the least
Opposition?" His heels
Click convulsively.
The colonels nod. His mind
Is clearly elsewhere.

Not there
But in the General's bed,
No Mata Hari, the English
Spy reclines. Miranda,
Pale and blue and yellow,
Her hair pressed to his
Pillow, her legs bare
Beneath the starched flat
Sheet, her breasts, arms,
Shoulders naked in the air,
His hollow room. Her teeth
Are small and round and sharp.

When will he move, arch a finger
On the map, alert the tanks
For a full advance? His eyes
Are closed, his pointer
Clatters to the floor. He sighs.

Her nervous tongue advances
The hollows of her lower
Lip, tips in and out.

A shout in the swirling sand,
The canvas rips as muzzles rise,
The general stalks the empty room,
His eyes lit, thoughts of the pass,
The plunging charge, the clash,
A grapple with the foe.

Bang, maps on the floor,
The double door snaps to,
A frightened aide,
The general in the sand
Who bellows in the wind,
Turns in the sand,
Stands in the turning sand.
He contemplates
A victory for the fatherland.

Her fingers tap his name
In Morse along her thigh,
Assault soon to begin,
Her job, his boots
Beyond the door.

A tank antenna whips
The wind.

       Another win,
Another loss, toss
Of the sheets from head
To toe. He knows
The maps, lay of the land

As pale Miranda
Watches his advance
And nips her thumb.

OUT OF SIGHT, OUT OF MIND

for John and Elizabeth Rodenbeck

The hawser parts, snap,
Stands erect. The ship,
The quay, the water and the dock
Are packed as the deck
Begins to tilt with the sea.

Was the banner green, or
Was it red? The queen, she
Wept, but the king had
A stiff upper lip. Mad
Cristobal or was it Cristoforo
Strode the crowd, with a shout
Cried out and the ship stood
Still.

A caravan, the camel fought
The driver's clothes, brought
The East to court, egged
The wild Italian forth:

The sail was crossed;
The sea was red.

And in her silken bed,
Spread like a cross herself,
In a pout, she lay, still
Warm from Columbo's breath.

At sea. To sea. The West
And spices of a golden
Land. Mad Cristobal
Forgets to wave good-bye.

from *NEWS OF THE NILE*

*The old people in a new world, the new people
made out of the old, that is the story that I
mean to tell, for that is what really is and
what I really know.*
                              — Gertrude Stein

*Meantime this earth of ours . . . is full
of wonders and mysteries and marvels, and
. . . it is good to go up and down seeing
and hearing tell of them all.*

                              — Rudyard Kipling

NIGHT OF THE UNDEAD

1.

*Her lips were never near the blood. The
tongue was relatively long. It moved at
the rate of about four darts a second.
At the instant of protrusion it was pinkish,
but once in action it functioned so
perfectly that a pulsating ribbon of blood
spanned the gap between the surface of the
fluid and the creature's lips.*

> — R. L. Ditmars & A. M. Greenhall
> "The Vampire Bat"

Adam's fall lies on you
Like your own arm in the night,
Dead with your weight,
Heavy as your dream,
You heave to throw it off.

You see it in all things:
The goat's hot blood
And randy eye, tail
Of the lizard, raven's
Croak, the buzzard's meal,

Erosion, drought,
The plague, the rain
That does not wash it clean,
Tree's knot, bare wood
That rots and warps,
The tumor and the wound,
Necessity of blood.

Smear yourself with the hoopoe's blood
And you will dream of smothering devils,
Drink the blood of the beast
And be as strong as his dark heart,
Swallow the leech
And he will drain you dry.

The sun sets like blood,
Rises like blood,
Dry clay is the color of dry blood,
Sap flows in the spring like blood,
You cry like bleeding,
Your blood is as black as loam,
You are swollen with blood,
Yearn for the lancet, the bleeding cup.

2.

> *And so I muddied the clear spring of
> friendship with the dirt of physical
> desire and clouded over its brightness
> with the dark hell of lust.*
>
> — St. Augustine
> *Confessions*

You are quiet as a snake
In winter, coiled,
Your eyes as clear
As gemstones, as cool.

Who would suspect?

Hunched over her small bed,
You would lick her veins dry,
Have her in the winding sheet,
Pale as potato stalks in the dark room,
Still as basalt, as carved granite.

Your teeth ache like your nerves,
Heart's muscular desire,
Down to the root, like a small boy
Chewing grass in the frenzy,
Like a fallen fruit
Splitting in the day's heat.

The reptile's scar on your heel,
Crippled, you crave the bat's wing,
The sweet smell of its gorged sleep,
Night vision, the quick tongue.

And if her eyes prove red
As her swollen lips,
Her teeth sharp to your throat,
Her touch like the vampire's kiss,
Thirsty for the same raw drink,
You will empty like a shadow,
Shrill as a north wind, cold
As the coffin, dirt to dirt,
Try to cry out your name
And scrabble on the floor at dawn.

3.

> *The last glimpse I had was of the bloated*
> *face, blood-stained and fixed with a grin*
> *of malice which would have held its own in*
> *the nethermost hell.*
>
> — Bram Stoker
> *Dracula*

You are howling like a dog,
You lick your own shame.

You are naked as a new day,
Shivering in the bright air.

The eye that stirred
Your pain is as common
As your own, as dull,
Her fingers, point
Of the hip, the wrist.

You are old meat,
Aware of each clogged cell,
The bruise that spreads
Beneath the skin,
Split tooth, shaved bone,
The liquid in your lungs.

Your lips are cracked
Like a dry river bed,
You are washed in blood,

Sluice of the pulse
That rushes in your ear,
Source of the open sore.

You dream of the coffin's lid,
The driven stake to cure
Your skinned heart, wolfsbane
And garlic, your head hacked off.

You are lonely as the lost wolf,
The slug, the blind whale.

A dove's feet are red
As fire, as spilled blood,
As its own hard eyes.

We once took hope
That the pelican was said
To feed its young
With its own red blood.

ACT OF DETECTION

Being singularly free from the conventional
sentimentalities and current superstitions,
he could look beneath the surface of human
acts into actuating impulses and motives.

— S. S. Van Dine

The centipede, the spider,
Shark's head and beetle's
Shell, disordered room,
The mind at bay, the mind.

The fact of Bela Kiss:
Scorpio and Cancer, knot
Of the strangling cord,
Two dozen dead, two dozen,
Broken and floating in oil,
Preserved like foetal pigs,
Their throats cracked
Like ice, naked, female,
Their hair like pond scum.

Pull back the curtain,
Probe in the new dust,
Examine the surfaces,
Chair rungs, the mirror's
Back, chalk out the floor,
Dry out the corners
Of the room, and pry,
Pry at the corners, the seams,
The ravelling paper on the wall.

Think of the guillotine,
The headsman's ax, the rack,
The wheel, the lives
Of the saints, the hangman's
Noose; remember loud Jack
The Ripper, quiet Kürten,
And the sane assassins,
Guiteau and Czolgosz,
Booth's dangling leg.

Measure and reflect,
Examine the stiffness
Of the arm, eye's cast,
The burn, the stain,
Mashed roach and spider's
Sting. The mind at bay.

The quick mind, quick
As the centipede, the shark's
Hard thrust, circling
The room, the room, circles
The room, wall, curtain
And door, closed door,
Locked door, shut window,
Circles and bumps the mirror,
And sees the eye, bared
Tooth, the quick grimace,
Skull in the mirror, face,
The mind at bay, the mind.

AFTER THE ELECTION, A DRY SEASON

Toad sweat and wart water,
Old blister, the pond
Shrunk to its thick center,
Its broken bank, snake holes,
The jerked frogs and hard scum.

The autumn ducks fly by
Sun bound and water true;
The white fowl are dead
In ragged weed and dry dirt.
This water holds no sky.

LOOKING FOR ASIA

You are out of the way to Japon,
for this is not it.
— Captain Luke Foxe (1631)

The bay is as cold
As colored silk at night,
As smooth as colored silk.

The two small ships hang
On their anchor lines
Like paper balloons,
Easing around in the tide,
Echoed in the still water.

Well into the long day,
The sun reaches for Japan
As it crosses the bay
And points the ships' masts
Back home across the water,
Across lost Vinland, the ocean,
The familiar tides of Bristol.

Captain Foxe offers his advice,
And the two captains laugh
Like the rattle of swords,
Tear the silent air
Like paper walls, secure
In having come beyond the point
Of Frobisher's return, where
Hudson's wake lingers
In the still cold water
Like an uneasy ghost.

We find the story
In *North-West Fox*, p. 223,
(1635). The captains' laughter
Eddies in the bay, mingles
With the sound of axes
On the shore, spattering
From the slim pines
Like small arms fire.

ON MYNYDD HIRAETHOG: AFTERNOON

for Ian & Kanta Walker

On Mynydd Hiraethog high near Llyn Alwen
Where the hill peels off from the stone tower
And the stained glass creaks in the dark house,
The wind cracks the air as you would crack an egg,
Splits and separates it, lays the flat grass flatter
And makes a man lean heavy, angle out.
The rain comes in level, and you must turn
The top of your cap into it like a round tweed shield.
The windscreen wipers of your car slip through,
Only lead you blind to the edge of the road
And the moor sliding off under the gravel.
Denbigh Castle was in friendly hands, safe
With wide boards laid on the damp shirred stone,
And the Vale of Llangollen will be still
With chimney smoke hanging low and steady,
But on Mynydd Hiraethog the storm
Stirs Llyn Alwen into stiff froth,
Winds the dim hallways of the stone house
Shrill with the afternoon, whips clouds
Into flat rain, and forces you to faith,
Leaning down to sunset on the wind.

DELIVERING THE MAIL

At first, it is a delicate task,
The sorting out, the spreading,
The tips of the fingers, light
And deft, the nerves alert,
Opening the box, always aware
Of appropriate zones, the necessary code.

When everything is properly out
And all directions are clear,
You must place the mail in the pouch,
Which you have oiled and rubbed,
Kept firm and soft, supple
Without losing its shape.

Lay it in carefully and in order,
Carelessness at this juncture
Can spoil an entire day's work,
Cancel the best of plans,
Everything in as it should be,
In to be taken out, all in good time.

And then the tour itself,
Steadily through the whole route,
Moving in and out of the pouch,
Separating and putting it in the slot,
Each piece in its place,
Each item delivered home.

And now you can relax,
A job well done, first class,
In spite of driving rain, the sleet
Or hail, the mail delivered,
The post gone through, at ease,
And the pouch stored safely away.

THE GLASS DOG

Quanto tempo resteremo qui?
— G. de Chirico

Clear air is following
A true line
And a low lining,
True air and a long validity.

Motion informs a locomotive
Before a low moon,
Limned clear and along,
Lunar and an eyelid.

Scene with a new eye:
Motor ability and a fall,
Formal, lunatic, allow
A rising of the moon.

And the cloud of steam
Lime green, reformed,
Or a true clarity,
Malleable and modern.

Angry under a clear moon,
I lead, and she, mad,
Alone, agreeing, meets
The locomotive, the urn.

The dun hand in a round air
Lining her and the city,
Mills, dams, the small sea,
And the moon a clear motion.

MOBILIZATION

The line of beauty symbolizes motion.
— Bronson Alcott

Invisible like old trees,
An arc of birds, the thermometer,
A face, the familiar curve,

Words make new lines,
Die like oiled mosquitoes,
Seldom turn to a proper circle.

A bare wall, brick, the mortar
Splitting like skin, the nerve
Spread in a raw frame,

A steady hand must know
The aim, a flowing, shape
Of the eye, rolling, still.

Around the wire the coiled foot
Must hold, the arms may wave,
The ear hear the pluckt tone,

But balance depends alone
On sea sounds of the inner ear,
Moon drawn, swollen, round.

A bomb's path to earth
Is as well the plane's away,
A bullet's, the pitched ball's,

Fired out or thrown,
Dropped, the line is one,
Change slow, curve of a tear.

Flat on the screen, a cheek
Is flesh to thought, a porcelain cube
Curves on a larger screen,

Is as hard and plane to eye
As concrete to the hand,
For mind pays no mind to fact.

Visible as love's touch,
The shout, cut tree, dead bird,
The opossum by the porch step,

Words make old lines
Revive like warm turtles,
Bend to realize a move.

NEWS OF THE NILE

Don't all rivers flow south, or is that
just a common misconception?

— Anonymous Student
Twentieth Century

1.
The river Nile flows north from Khartoum,
Blue and white. Two rivers meet at Khartoum,
Mix between Tuti and Omdurman day and night
And flow north to wine-dark seas, past these:

2.
Towns of the Nile:
Khartoum, trunk of the elephant, Atbara,
Fagrinkotti, Dongola, Kerma and Wawa;
Names now lost in Nasser's lake (Gebel Adda,
Dakka, Kabosh and Kalabsha); Aswan
And Kôm Ombo, Luxor and Thebes, Sohâg
And Mallawi, Biba, Badahl and Beni Suef;
Khartoum, where the Mahdi rules,
To Maadi where John Rodenbeck resides;
And, too, the delta's many jumbled towns.

3.
The fat man wears a tarboosh
Though his head seems made for fez.
He is standing at the elevator's doors.
He claps his hands and claps them
Once again. The only sound
That circles down the shaft
Is Fakkaruni. Um Kalsum is on
The radio.

4.
Cairo is a city of tall buildings,
Martian by a crow's choice, city
Red in the late sunlight, the Citadel
And Cairo Tower in the setting sun.
The taxis blow their horns. The Nile
Makes islands in its northern way.

5.

The music's high and loud, it has
No count in decibels, dark glasses
And hot coffee in the bar. The voice
Is Um Kalsum's. A fat man pauses
At the door and tilts his head.
The song is Fakkaruni. The sun is hot.
Dark glasses for the light is needle bright.

6.

The Nile flows north. A train runs north
From Roanoke to Chicago. The snow
Is like cold satin. There is a gibbous moon.
North to Chicago, towards Minnesota
Where the Mississippi oozes from a frozen bank
And wanders south, to Wisconsin
Where August Derleth prints the books
Of Lovecraft, dreamer of *The Book of Thoth*,
The Necronomicon, lost work of Abdul Alhazred,
Lovecraft who wrote of Nug and Dagon,
Old gods, Nÿogtha and Cthulhu.
And east of this train, south of Virginia,
In western North Carolina, Fred Chappell
Has written a novel, *Dagon*, and all these things
Come together, turn together, and will pass on
To come again. The Nile flows sluggish
And is thick with mud. It bears the news.

7.

The Nile has other names:
Kasumo and Kagira, Mukasenyi,
Ruvironza and Kagera, Nilus
And Ruvabu. The Nile, white and blue.

8.

A fat man in Chicago buys a ticket,
Walks into the darkness and sits down.
The Mummy's Curse is on a double bill,
The Mummy's Curse of 1944. The mummy,
His one hot eye that sees the ends of things,
Is Lon Chaney, and the fat man sweats
With fear, thinks of George Zucco,
Turhan Bey and Carradine. His palms

Are wet as Kharis seeks his revenge.
Anck-es-en-amon could live again;
Imhotep disguised as Ardath Bey
Attempts to steal her into life,
Worships Anubis, his jackal head,
But is destroyed by Isis, her potent rod.
The Mummy (1932), with Boris Karloff,
As the fat man clutches his left arm
And gasps. The Nile flows north,
Its banks weighted with temples,
Drinking the mud of their foundations.

9.

Gods of the old Nile, there are these:
Nun and Atum, Ra, Anhur and Shu,
Osiris, his wife Isis who is mother
Of all things (or was), Hathor who fed
Young Amenhotep as a cow, and falcon
Horus, Anubis and the baboon Thoth.
These and others, cat-headed Bast,
And Hapi (not Hapy, son of Horus,
But the dual goddess of the Nile),
All these and more. God bless
The reader of these names.

10.

The moon is high as the Nile is slow.
The snow is melting now in the dead
Of winter, but spring is still far away.
All these things I have read and remembered,
Witnessed, imagined, thought and written down,
Having ridden north on trains by day and night
With Henry Taylor to read our poems, listened
To recordings of Um Kalsum, dreamed of the Nile
And the moon dancing in dry palm fronds,
I, Richard Dillard, in this month of February 1967.

DOWNTOWN ROANOKE: 1967

1.

The streetlights blink DONT WALK WALK
DONT WALK and the cars are filling
The air with burnt gas. And all will pass.
I often think and secretly suspect
Big Lick will come again and cows
Will graze in downtown Roanoke.

2.

A trip to the zoo: where we watch
The llamas chew and stare, stare
At the bears and pat the baby goats.
We walk by the crazy mirrors
Where we are stranger than the strangers
In the cages, furry and climbing
On the wire of their cages.
We ride the small train and wave
Out over the edge of the mountain,
Wave down at the valley, the puzzle
Of downtown Roanoke.

3.

The star on the mountain turns red
Whenever someone dies in the street,
But I have heard (although I have not seen)
That late at night in the earliest
Of morning, someone always turns
It red and then, I wonder, does
Someone gasp and stumble into a car
And die in downtown Roanoke?

4.

The mayor puffs on his cigar,
(The mayor is my dad), puffs
On his cigar, and the children
Dance around his legs, they sing
And toss petals in the smoky air,
And the mayor puffs on his cigar,
(The mayor is my dad), while people
Stare, he puffs, the little ones,
They dance and sing, the people

On the sidewalks think it strange, they
Do not understand in downtown Roanoke.

5.
From the airport the whisper jet
Rises on a wisp of black smoke
And a thunderous roar, draws me
To the door to observe. It is
A pale night and the lights
Of the plane are blinking green
And red. The star is white.
And the jet flies on while
The moon is full, as I think
Seriously of climbing in my car
And driving down 581 to see
The empty streets of downtown Roanoke.

6.
The Park and the Roanoke
And even the Rialto are parking
Lots. The Academy of Music
With its famed acoustics
Where Caruso and others sang
Is long down and gone.
There are many parking lots
And garages in downtown Roanoke.

7.
The Pakistani gentleman said,
In progress to a nearby college,
"I have lived in the vale of Kashmir
For much of my life, but I would
Gladly live and die in this valley."
The valley is green, the mountains blue,
All around downtown Roanoke.

8.
The furniture store across the street
From the main firehouse has burned
Nearly to the ground three times.
The smoke hung low and red, the red
Stoplights blinked, but no sirens
Were required in downtown Roanoke.

9.
And when it rains, it pours water
In streams down the windows of the stores
And blurs the names, and down the windshields
Of heavy trucks and delivery vans. It wets
Down the dust and cleans the air and wets
The trainmen's high striped hats, makes
All the highways slick, and pours
Down all the undertakers' black umbrellas.
When it rains, the water runs down
The tombstones in each of the various cemeteries
And wears down the stone and wears down
The names into the ground where their dust
Lies. And when it rains, it wets the sides
Of buildings, and the building by the tracks
Built out of coal sheds long black streams
That crawl across the sidewalk, streak the gutters,
And run down the streets of downtown Roanoke.

10.
There was once a pool hall one flight
Down across the street from another
One just one flight up. The lower
One had a sign that read BILLIARDS.
The higher one is still there, one
Flight above downtown Roanoke.

11.
There are a great many birds in Roanoke.
I have seen: a great blue heron,
A green heron, the shy least bittern,
Orioles and robins, killdeers
Live near my house, and sandpipers,
Cowbirds who pick the dung of cows,
Wrens and sparrows, the familiar
Cardinals and blue jays, martins
And swallows, warblers make the air
Yellow in the spring, grackles,
A hundred cedar waxwings my mother found
Eating berries in a dogwood tree,
And towhees, nighthawks, and high
Overhead, their wings ragged
And spread wide, vultures, black
And circling over downtown Roanoke.

12.
My dog is from Georgia. My friends
Are from New York and South Carolina,
Florida, Texas and northern Virginia,
Norfolk and even Connecticut.
My grandparents and parents
Are all from south of here,
From Franklin and Henry counties.
Sometimes it seems I am the only native,
That all the other inhabitants
Are castaways in downtown Roanoke.

13.
At early dusk in Roanoke the lights go on,
Neon, they're red and green, are purple,
Never gold, blink, stammer and fizz,
And say the names of things to people
Driving through, walking the streets,
On Pullmans in the railway yards
Waiting for the porter to make their beds.
The sign for YELLOW CAB is red and shines
Through white smoke to make the center
Of the city blaze like the mouth of hell
At early dusk. And outside the light
With only one red neon light at night,
The topless go-go girls lift up their knees,
They shake their breasts and do the frug
And bugaloo, they never smile, dance
In the dark beyond the light in downtown Roanoke.

14.
There is a blind lady with tilting
Scales on the seal and flag of Roanoke,
With steaming railroad trains
Shuffling at her knees. She appears
To be a young lady, and there is a great
Cogwheel or gear beside her.
The flag is blue. When they took
The one in the Council chambers
Down to make a copy, it fell
Into many pieces. One small piece
With one full pan of the blind lady's
Scales flew out of the window,

Across the lawn and into the traffic
Grinding gears in downtown Roanoke.

15.
We are watching the night, and the wind
Is very high. It strums the TV antenna.
It blows the dog's ears and makes
The windows rattle. The large highway
Signs hum in the wind. It makes
The heavy neon and steel star shake.
Perhaps it will accidentally turn
Red. It blows around and all round
The valley, wrinkling the new pale
Leaves on the trees, blowing
An occasional bird's nest over
And scattering the eggs. The wind
Blows up the streets and slaps
A bus transfer against the window
Of an elementary school principal's
House. She stops grading papers
And thinks of calling the police.
It rattles a paper cup up Jefferson
Street from the viaduct, a right
Turn onto Campbell Avenue, wrong
Way onto a one-way street, turns left
On First Street at Fine's Men's Shop
And passing Kirk winds up in a storm
Drain at the corner of First and Church.
The wind blows the flat metal signs
On the side streets, blows grit
Into a rookie policeman's eyes.
He almost draws his gun but instead
Steps into the pool hall door. It blows
All up and down the streets, moans
In the halls of the empty office
Buildings, rattles the mayor's door,
And the door of my dentist next door,
And the door of the Office of Smoke Control.
The wind blows the mercury vapor lamps
That keep it always light in downtown Roanoke.

TRAVELOGUE

for Henry Taylor

There are things I have seen
Although I have not been
To where they are. They burst
In my skull like instant coffee
Flavor buds. My eyes spin
Like firework wheels, crackle
Like Frankenstein's machines.
I am ecstatic and grow
Electrically happy like cat's fur
Rubbed briskly backwards.

SALT LAKE

A little corner of Utah is soon traversed,
and leaves no particular impressions on
the mind.

— Robert Louis Stevenson

Where the mind tries to sink
But cannot, bobs up, dizzy,
Crusty, wrinkled, crystalline.

Afloat on the Salt Lake,
Feet crossed, exposed
Like confused icebergs,
Head back on a pillow
Of salt water, half asleep,
Dreaming of saline spectra
And the true way west . . .

The cut on your lip
Stings like the memory
Of rain; the locusts
Whir and split
Like late summer hail.
The seagulls scrape
As they circle
The encircled monument.

I have come in search
Of Eldorado which my friend
Poe indicated might be here
Where all the gold is soft
As lead and pure white.

You look vainly for waves,
Kick, crawl, stroke, scratch
Your skull on the hard water.

And then to awaken,
To wake up and take off,
Make the flat way to Nevada,
To Oasis, Deeth, Beowawe
And Lovelock.

And discover
That the gray surface
Of your mind is as smooth
As a balloon blown past
All trace of pucker.

THE UNKNOWN ESKIMO

These lonely latitudes do not belong
to the habitable world.
            — Eugene Sue

The ground stiffens
Like arteries, trees
Like old toes, hard joints,
A wind shadowing the leaves
Across the day. Dead insects
Sting the sill. Light fails.

You feed the fire pages
Of last week's news, today's,
The wood damp as last week,
Cold as today.

North of Anaktuvuk, east
Of Point Barrow, the ice shifts
Like a dreaming animal,
Settles, solid as the soil,
As the sea below.

The sky is as lost
As the *Erebus* and the *Terror*.
The day disappears.

Think of the breath
Of caribou which hangs
For hours in the rigid air,
Of the unknown eskimo,
Of the polar bear, white
On a white plain, scenting
The hard white air.

HOMAGE TO GERTRUDE STEIN

The asparagus
Is a green fountain
Through the open doorway,
Moving in the same air
That thrills the warm hair
Of your bare arm.

Here is a photograph:
First, the barbed point,
Honing the green grass,
Then the living shaft,
An unsupported spire.

And after slow rain,
A silent rush
And green mist.

This single photograph,
This open doorway.

MEDITATION FOR A PICKLE SUITE

Morning: the soft release
As you open a jar of pickles.
The sun through the window warm
And moving like light through brine,
The shadows of pickles swim the floor.
And in the tree, flowing down the chimney,
The songs of fresh birds clean as pickles.
Memories float through the day
Like pickles, perhaps sweet gherkins.
The past rises and falls
Like curious pickles in dark jars,
Your hands sure as pickles,
Opening dreams like albums,
Pale Polish pickles.
Your eyes grow sharp as pickles,
Thoughts as green, as shining
As rows of pickles, damp and fresh,
Placed out in the afternoon sun.

THE MULLINS FARM

The sun through the window
Is as warm as the smell of salt,
Of hams, the hum of bees
Where the smoke bellows lie
On the table by the netting,
The hat and the gloves.

My uncle hands you a turtle's heart,
Beating, beating in your open hand,
His head still hooked on the broom,
The hollow of his bones on the ground,
And his parts laid out by the fire,
The kettle made ready for soup.

The high horse, Mack, dappled white,
And the brown, too, slow and full,
The hill that falls off from the barn
Where the corn is husked in the dark,
And the hogs hanging to be split,
Filled with apples and corn and sweet slop.

By the branch out back and the small bridge,
In the damp concrete walls, the milk
Sits in spring water, and the squares
Of pressed butter, each with its bouquet
Of spring flowers, and on the bank,
An occasional frog or small snake.

The horseshoes must be bent on hot coals,
Red and white as new flowers, sprinkled
On the ground around the anvil, inviting
To your hand which must never touch,
And the shadows of the waiting horses,
The hot hammers, the hard men.

And the red hen in your arms is soft
And warm as the smell of feathers,
As the afternoon, while a small hawk
Watches from a crooked pine, watches
My grandfather in his clean tan clothes
Load his shotgun in the porch's shade.

And my grandmother rings the wood stove,
Takes the biscuits from the high warmer,
Calls her daughters to set the table,
And feeds the large family with squirrel
And green beans, squash and mashed potatoes,
As a brace of dead crows hang from the fence.

The afternoon is unending and clear
As the branches in front of and behind
The white house, as you climb the hill
To the barn, smell the stacked hay,
Touch the smooth wood of the stalls,
And see the sun powdered by barn dust.

My grandfather has cut a log of green wood
And set it up in the fireplace
With dry props to light as the evening
Comes on, and you may sit in the dim room
With the shadows wrinkling your face,
Hear the fire living in the light's slow leak.

The hounds are asleep on the front porch,
Their flat brown ears and sharp ribs,
While the cats climb to eat on a fence post,
And the oaks rattle acorns in the grass
And on the tin roof of the porch,
And the corn stalks crack in the air.

A DAY, A COUNTRY HOME

Homage to Vladimir Nabokov

This true estate:

There is time here for the sea
To die in waves slow as eyes,
Where the sound of each dying
Holds to the ear like hunger.

You walk along the pebbles
Of the shore. The high leaves
Lap at the late sun like dogs
Hot from the romp, the chase.

The water moves like a freed circle,
Spiralling into froth, into foam,
As the stone darkens and gleams
At each departure, wave on wave.

Is there a house through the trees,
Catching light through the leaves
Like butterflies, like the sun
Too bright to see, like the day?

You see two figures far down the shore,
A young man, a younger woman,
Examining the stones, pocketing
A few bright pebbles, watching you.

The sun touches the edge of the day
As gingerly as hands, as fingers,
Your shadow slips long into the aspens,
Into their shade, clear to the golden walls.

A POETRY OF THE ACT

for W. R. Robinson

It's like riding a hot horse
Into high breakers, foam
On foam. You are wet
Through and through, and thrown
By horse and sea, laid out
On the sand, pushed in,
The undertow sucks only
At your feet and knees, winded,
Dazed, happy, as the horse
Stands shivering by the piled rocks.

from *AFTER BORGES*

No true composer will take his substance from another
finite being — but there are times when he feels that
his self-expression needs some liberation from at least a part
of his own soul. At such times, shall he not better turn
to those greater souls, rather than to the external,
the immediate, and the 'Garish Day'?

— Charles Ives

SWEET STRAWBERRIES

Like wet windows
On an open day. Skin knows.

The color punctuates
The shadows, the patches
Of hot sun.

No bitter core, the vine
Knows the ground
Like grass.

The taste lingers
Like touch.

Like leopards' eyes
Ignite the trees
Around the fire.

This I know:

Who loves me.

WINGS

A celebration:

The wings of a bird, a shadow
That severs a bright day
Leaving it bright, a sparrow's
Wing, sooty, a sooty tern's,
Bright and white as the day
The sparrow split, a hawk's,
An eagle's, a wren's,
Wings that iron the air
And ring the ear, birds.

A package of cigarettes
With a card enclosed, .
A shiny P-40 (more wings)
Against a blue and birdless
Sky, a wing of new smoke.

A trip to the moon.

The last two crisp wings
Beside the lonely neck
In the platter at the center
Of Sunday's spattered table,
The napkins crumpled
And greasy, scattered
On the linen like wings.

The wings of angels
Bending low.

The invisible wings of insects
Confusing the eye, evading
The swallow, the phoebe,
Scattered across the sill,
Along the sunny floor,
A dry variety of veins.

Dawn's wing, day's wing,
Wing of the eye that folds
The day to sleep, wing

Of the flying fish, the squirrel,
Wing of your house, your chair,
Of the stage, of the weather vane,
Wing of the maple's fruit,
Of the ash, the organ of flight,
An extension of the mind.

Winging it.

THE SECOND DEATH

Breaking out of ground
Like fire, like weeds
Nodding in the early air,
Like water on a still day.

The dead are uneasy
And difficult, swaying
Over the rowboat's stern,
The long gray hair tangled
As if by wind, the mouth
Open to speak, to say
Eye's leak, the open ear.

When the storms start
And swell the waters
Behind the dam, the stones
May well part, and in their dark canoes
The dead will sweep down river.

What is King Canute's surprise
Beside this? The dead
Are touring the day.

LES OMBRES ARTIFICIELLES

Homage to Alain Robbe-Grillet

De nouveau la scène est vide.

The light as diffuse and bright
As light, a corridor marked
By the interruption of doors,
Of the knobs of doors,
Each one as bright and precise
As light, one window
At the far end of the corridor,
The quick stutter of doors.

The light as diffuse and dim
As light, a corridor blurred
By the interruption of doors,
Of the knobs of doors,
Each one as dim and precise
As light, one window
At the far end of the corridor,
The dull progression of doors.

The light as acute and bright
As light, a corridor cut
By the interruption of doors,
Of the knobs of doors,
Each one as bright and approximate
As light, one window
At the far end of the corridor,
The deadly accuracy of doors.

Once more the scene is empty.

THE OTHER TIGER

(After the Spanish of Jorge Luis Borges)

"And the craft that createth a semblance, and fails of the heart's desire;
And the toil that each dawning quickens and the task that is never done,
And the heart that longeth ever, nor will look to the deed that is won."

Reading Morris, you think of a tiger,
The living coal of fire. The dark library
Expands, large and alive, larger, the shelves
Push back; excessive, innocent, tawny and tangerine,
The tiger, blooded and new, will walk
Through its jungle, will sink its tracks
In the river's wet bank, a river whose name
It will not know (a world and moment
Without name or time), will walk wild ways,
Will scent in the woven wind sweet dawn and deer.
In the partings of the bamboo you discover
The sharp stripes of its hair, feel
The bones hard through the hot hide.
A world curves, water and sand, in vain;
In the lost south, South America,
You dream the tiger you trace,
"O tiger on the banks of the Ganges."

The afternoon spreads like a soul,
Your soul as you reflect that the tiger
To whom you just spoke in this poem
Is only symbols and shadows, memories
From the encyclopedia, literary turns,
No deadly tiger, no fatal jewel
Under the Sumatran sun, moon of Bengal,
A round of love and laziness and death.
You have set against this symbolic beast
The real thing, the tiger of warm blood,
Hungry for buffalo, heedless of horn,
That stretches in the high grass today,
The third of August, 1959 (and today,
20th of March, 1970), and today, a shadow at rest,
Still and quiet by the act of its naming,
Already the fiction of your thought,
No living tiger breathing the air of the earth.

We shall search out a third tiger:
Like the others stretched out in this poem,
The form of our dreaming, shape of our words,
Man-made, spineless, not the quick tiger
That knows and stalks the days beyond all myth.
What drives us from the grasses into the trees,
Drives us to this hunt, this empty hunt,
Ancient and absurd? We press on, blind
In the late afternoon, hunting the other tiger,
The one who is never in a poem.

ANOTHER TIGER

Homage to Jorge Luis Borges

In Buenos Aires, the first tiger:
Delicate in the river mud,
Marking a sharp line
On the border
Of land and water.

We know the river's name,
More than the tiger knows.

Still he walks there
By the river.

He does not stop to drink.

The second tiger:
A real one, hungry and hot,
This one in India
After buffalo.

It hangs soon in the rooms of your mind
However,
Tanned in the heat of your name.

Another:

A jaguar perhaps, circles within circles
On its tawny hide, hung in a tree
Over the trail.

The sun conspires with the leaves
To hide him from your eyes.

You return to Buenos Aires,
To the library by the silver river.

Tigers and tigers haunt its stacks.

The jaguar licks its fur
And lolls in the sheltering leaves.

MAP

But even with imaginary places, he will
do well in the beginning to provide
a map. As he studies it, relations
will appear that he had not thought upon.

— Robert Louis Stevenson

A map with a scale of 3 English miles
Held against the sea by mermaids,
Their breasts salty and bare,
Their hair slick as a seal:

Fish lie on the waves, mouths
Open like gills to the air,
As birds burst from the sea,
Row into the air and fly.

The land is broken by swamps
And graves (the bones' slow rot
In the damp, loose earth). South
Of the island there is foul ground,
Too, where rocks break the water
Like hungry fish, like birds.
A strong tide sucks the western shore.

The ship lies in 10 fathoms
Off the narrow spit
Where white rock stands
Like a raw statue. Gulls
Swing out from the stone
Like flat rocks skipping
Low across the water
And circle the masts,
Crying like fish on the waves,
Crying like mermaids at night.

Lines solid and broken
Sweep out from the compass
Like broken glass, slice
Through the water
And under the land,

Tie sea and soil together
Like a spyglass swung slowly
From west to north to east.

The moon draws at the tide.
Skeletons of fish slide
On the sand to the roots of trees.
Gulls mutter in their sleep
And dream of the rising sea.
The mermaids hold against the tide,
Their tails splashing in the moon,
A scale of 3 English miles.

A WORLD

El anverso y el reverso de esta moneda
son, par Dios, iguales.

Borges speaks of a world
Of bored barbarity, of monotonous
Savagery, of dull cruelty.

True enough.

He continues
But the world remains.

A leg breaks lazily,
Splitting the long way
Like the branch of a walnut
With the weight of ice.

In the dark building
They tie you to a chair
And edge you, straining,
To the edge of the stairs.

The long rows blur
To a grey serpent, sliding
Crookedly across the mud,
The chains lashing
Like ground teeth,
Sharp as your fear,
The water of your nerve.

The prevalence of blood,
Spreading on the highway,
Pooling in the sour cellar,
Draining under the locked door,
A heart pumps wildly
Into the stained air.

Words that strike
Like shaggy spears, like stones,
Like short, honed swords,
The quiet words that stick

In the comfortable air
Like clumsy darts.

The eyes of animals swell
In their heads, their lips
Tug nervously back, hackles
Stiff as dry blood. A wind
Rises and clatters the dark wood.
Grasses snarl in the clearing.
Rain stings like lead pellets.
The walls of the house strain
Like foundering ships.

Your side cracked like a husk,
Jesus, sprayed the soldier's
Face with blood and water:

Cracked like graves
With the bodies of waking saints,
Like rent garments,
Like the rotten temple wall:

Cracked like dry skin,
Dry dirt around the base
Of the skull:

Cracked like a caul,
Like the sweet taste
Of walnuts, of water,
Cracked like parting waters,
Like the scales of a new bud
Hot in the darkened air.

WHEEL

Siempre se pierde lo esencial.

Perhaps carved in stone,
Its spokes rigid as the four fixed signs
Of the zodiac, on the chariot
Of an Assyrian king, his ridged beard
Formal as the spokes, or of a pharaoh
Drawn by lean horses, their front feet
Multiplied by two, by four,
Carved in the air,
In all their hurry, in stone.

Or in silver on film,
Spinning backwards as the coach
Picks up speed, spilling dust
Down the center of town,
Slowing down and reversing
Like an electric fan
On a gusty day, stopping
In the dust that rises and falls
Like shadows on film in silver.

Or a captain lashed in a storm,
Hung on the rungs like a side of beef,
His daughter, salty and stiff,
Tied to the broken mast, the rudder
Beating the waves to the consistency
Of foam, of the little girl's hair
Spun out like frayed canvas,
Of the smoking sea in a storm.

Borges speaks of a circular delirium,
Of an encompassing circle, of circular
Ruins, of the zero, the cipher, coin
Like a crystal egg, cat's eye.

The harsh jackal's head of Anubis
Grins like a dog over a gnawed bone,
Its spine shivered with selfish hair.
The calm face of the sphinx
Is a mirror to the empty air.

If fortune is a wheel,
What is a wheel?

RAIN

(After the Spanish of Jorge Luis Borges)

The afternoon produces a rain.

It also falls in the past.

You hear it. You remember the day
You first saw the color of a rose,
Saw the flower (you knew the name).

This rain closes the window,
But it opens tiny lenses in the screen
Of the room you knew, slicks the plums
On a bent tree that is no more.

This wet afternoon brings you the sound
You have been listening for:

Your father's voice, alive in the rain.

THREE FRIENDS

1. DUFY

Dufy's head settles securely in his collar.
Nature, he said, is only an hypothesis.
His striped tie signifies no school.

Dufy in a small white car in 1929:
He looks out of the rear window
Over the fat spare tire.
He misses, then, the large green car
Just ahead, and the Casino at Nice,
But he sees a blue bush, a green bush,
Someone in blue making a blue sketch.

In 1925 while they are playing jazz,
Dufy sees Hélène's arm, poised
Like an epaulet on Paul's shoulder.

It is necessary, he said, to create
A world of things that one does not see.

The smoke of the blue train is as blue
As grass. My favorite nude is there.
Dufy has just stepped back for a look,
Only a band of blue on his canvas.
The sun in the green sky is as warm
On her skin as Dufy's hand
If he were there.

Like music or a poem, he said, art
Is a creation. Dufy hums the Mozart blues.

2. LEGER

Léger's cap is a little large.
Machine made, it fits him
Like a halo or a glove.

Léger watches a building
Sprout from the earth
Like a locust, a weed

At first, wooding upward,
A tall tree, bending
In high winds, blooming.

Léger knows who made each machine
And each machinist.

On a picnic, he tinkers
With the motor of the odd car
While we touch each other
With the delicacy of mechanics.
The dog takes his ease
In the shade of Léger's coat,
Hung like a blossom on the tree.

Léger sees the city,
How buildings reflect
The angles of builders,
How smoke balloons
Over an engine,
How that man is constructed
Like a fine machine.

To see, hear, and touch,
Léger said, a multitude
Of things. He grins
Like a clown with a banjo.
He doffs his hat
With happy precision,
Like a flower
Wound up with keys.

3. TURNER

Turner's gaze is steady.
You want to turn away,
Turn it off like a light.

To an open eye, the elements
Fuse, fire, water and air
As parliament burns in oil,
The sun writhing like a water snake
As the sun sets in the Thames,

Earth, air, fire and water one
As parliament burns in watercolor,
To Turner's open eye.

Turner leans from the railway coach,
His head blurred in the fast rain,
Only a shower in a blue sky,
And he sees a boat on the river,
Picnickers, the black smokestack
And the black smoke sliding
Down the traincars in the rain.

I did not paint it to be understood,
Turner said, but I wished to show
What such a scene was like.

Turner watches a German mountain
Paint itself with the sunset,
Pale in the evening air
Across the fading water. He sees
How even a sea monster is swallowed
By sunrise, how light ages and changes,
How the shape of the world
Is the shape of an eye.

HOMAGE TO HENRY GREEN

It was no more or less, really,
Than we had expected:
Rose after rose after rose
Beyond a roadway asphalted blue,
The blood colored brick,
The young man in pink tweeds;

Or the nervous butler
With two very different eyes.

It is all in a manner of seeing.

He sees music like maids
In a ballroom. He sees
Fear like a dead pigeon.
He sees walls split like chestnuts
In the fire and burn the blue streets.

And he knows the limits of love:
Desire, memory, an end like suttee.

The afternoon slows silently
Into evening like music,
Like fear, like fire.

His eyes are warm
Like coals in a grate.
He sees the room sway
To the music of the fire.
He is safe and sure
In the boundaries of love.

No more, no less, really,
Than we had expected.

AMERICA IS DARKEN'D

Washington, Franklin, Paine & Warren, Gates, Hancock & Green

— William Blake

"Now, my dear friend, what is our plan?"
Cornwallis wrote to Phillips,
Already tired of Greene and Guilford,
Soon to leave with no reply
For Yorktown and Washington,
De Rochambeau and Comte de Grasse.

How could he know how Washington
Burned in the imagination of Blake,
How red hairy Orc squeezes out of earth
Like a tough vine to bloom in Yorktown?

Children, their clothes shed
Like worn skin, ride the tamed serpent,
As relaxed as fat lambs.

The *Terrible* blazes off Cape Charles.
Pale women burn in the flames, swell
Like new grapes on the vine, spread
Their legs and fly like smoke
Across Cape Charles, across Yorktown,
Darkening the blue mountains,
The dim midwest, the Rockies
Where the sun burns down like a pyre,
Like a ship hissing down in salt water.

What could Cornwallis do?
He and his armies fared better
In India where the fire was unreal,
Where the elephants kneeled on command,
Where dark men were used to Juggernaut
And could agree to the benefits of the wheel.

Lord North cried, "O God! It is all over!"

In America, Blake's dream burns on.
The smoke stings the eye to tears.

A YELLOW ROSE

(After the Spanish of Jorge Luis Borges)

Laid out in bed, near
The end, the old writer,
This new Homer, new Dante,
His room over a garden,
Marble, laurels, step after step,
Down to a pool doubling the day,
The laurels, the marble,
Step after step, he sees:

A yellow rose.

The woman has placed it
In his goblet by the bed.

He speaks his piece,
Lines as smooth and familiar
As the carved posts of the bed:
Porpora de' giardin, pompa de' prati,
gemma di primavera, occhio d'aprile . . .

He sees it:

A yellow rose, his eye edenic,
Open as Adam's,
A yellow rose.

His words do not hold it
Like a goblet. It is itself.
We may, he sees, allude to a rose
Or name a rose. We may, he knows,
Never say a rose at all.

The gold of his books on the shelf
Glows like a mirror. They are
No mirror, he sees, to the world.
They are only another item in it.

This light found Giambattista Marino
Like a knife before he died.

Perhaps it opened Homer's eyes
As well, was like a pinpoint small
As it is bright to Dante, too.

MORE TIGERS, DREAMTIGERS

(After the Spanish of Jorge Luis Borges)

> *We might contrive a very poetical and very*
> *suggestive ... philosophy, by supposing that*
> *the virtuous live while the wicked suffer*
> *annihilation, hereafter; and that the danger of*
> *the annihilation ... might be indicated nightly*
> *by slumber .... In proportion to the dreamlessness*
> *of the sleep, for example, would be the degree*
> *of the soul's annihilation.*
> — Edgar A. Poe

As a boy you lived tigers,
Asiatic tigers, royal and aloof,
In zoos, in books, approached
By cautious elephants with slit ears,
Castled with warriors.

You still remember them every one:
They replace days, faces, the smiles of women.

And they return nightly in the shadows
Of your dreams.

You are sleeping; a dream leads you astray.
You know you are dreaming. You think:
I am dreaming, a pure diversion of my will.
You hold power without limits.
You will cause a tiger to be.

Good bungler, no tiger appears.
Oh, a tiger does arrive, a stuffed tiger,
Or a gentle one, one with too long a tail
Or brown eyes, one as large as an elephant,
A flash of fur in the leaves, no danger,
A tiger that wags its tail and barks,
Or sings on a limb like a small yellow bird.

A TIGER YOU MAY HAVE MISSED

A tiger a rapt and surrounded overcoat securely
arranged with spots old enough to be thought
useful and witty quite witty in a secret and
in a blinding flurry.
— Gertrude Stein

This one as simple as a blanket,
Worn, warm, cut out of words
Like pinks and cool red roses.

What happened: a tiger in alphabets,
Arranged securely, safe as bars,
An old tiger put out on view,
Open as an eye to the eye.

A tiger, bluntly put, placed,
Set, practical and sure,
But your eye still wraps itself
In awe, in sharp surprise.

Then the tiger, hermetic, secret,
Blends in, disappears in lines,
In spots, in flurries of the eye,
Sudden, deadly, silent,
Lost to your thought, wound
In your eye, invisible in words.

You start again, again
The tiger disappears; again,
Again. But he grows familiar,
You know his trick and watch
Him go, like a blanket wearing out,
An overcoat, a shoe, a rose,
A tiger by the river, in the zoo.

EPILOGUE

(After the Spanish of Jorge Luis Borges)

> *The exchange which is fanciful and righteous*
> *and mingled is in the author mostly in the piece.*

— Gertrude Stein

You set out to shape a world.
Years pass: stones, wind in grass,
Mountains, the echoes of bays,
Waves, the stirring of tides,
Kingdoms, republics, states
Of the mind, old walls and scrolls,
Ships and sailors, sheets and sails,
Fishes, finny and fast, and sharks,
Rooms, closets, the cellar stairs,
Instruments and tools, knives, stars,
Horses and horsemen, women, men.

And then at the end, before you die,
You examine the maze of careful lines
To find there a face, wearing
And worn, warm as worn stone,
A face you know: your own.

CONSTRUCTION

*It seems that the human mind has first to
construct forms independently before we can
find them in things.*
— Albert Einstein

Vladimir Tatlin's demand:
Real materials in real space,

Solid and silent, an art of iron,
Of concrete, cut wood and glass.

A response: to say as you see,
Words set firm like a jaw.

The descent into silence. An ascent.
You breathe as you sleep, you circulate.

To say as you see. To see as by stop-action,
Clouds coil overhead, the passage of days,

Trees bend by the side of the road
Like tires on a curve, plants uncurl,

How the world dissolves in the water of the eye:
The illusion speed produces. The reality of speed.

A result: to see as you say,
As gravity may bend a ray of light.

To say the earth's center is of fire:
Life leaps from the soil like sun flares.

To see the world made true,
An art of rocks and stones and trees,

Real materials in real space,
L'esthétique de la vitesse.

THREE MORE FRIENDS

1. RYDER

It is hard to see Ryder sometimes
For the light, solid as trees,
It breaks through his worried eyes
And the orchard turns to light,
You could touch it, squeezed out
As from a tube, lighter than the eye
Recalls, cracking under the strain,
Better than nature, Ryder said,
The thrill of a new creation.

Ryder is a young man in a field,
Like a colt let loose, he said,
Learning to see how a field
Is a fold of the sky, with no details
To vex the eye, earth and leaves
And sky. He bellowed for joy.

Ryder in the Forest of Arden
Is as hard to see as lovers,
The trees like clouds, the clouds
Leaning on the air like trees,
And Ryder watches the day pass
In his eyes, trying to find, he said,
Something out there beyond the place
On which I have a footing.

Ryder at sea, Ryder at morning,
Ryder dreaming the history of the mind,
The witches lost in a shadow,
The moon burning like the point of a match
Through paper, the clouds singed,
The witches lost in shadow,
The sails of ships shaping the air
Like pyramids or tornadoes,
And Christ glows like a moon or a sun.

There is surprise in Ryder's face
When he looks at you, or recognition,
And you see shadows in his eyes
And a light as solid as trees.

2. HOMER

He is as solid as a businessman,
His collar etches his neck like acid,
A flower shedding in his buttonhole,
Homer, with a moustache like a brush,
Sprayed out and stiff, scrawled.

But a wave kisses the moon
And you know what it is to live
In water, or light as air on rapids,
Or broken as sand on a beach.
Just *look* at it! Homer said,
And color washes the eye like a dawn,
Or air, or sea water that scalds.

Homer at Prouts Neck,
Buttoned up, stiff as an easel,
Will not meet your eye,
But the Gulf Stream cracks
Over his shoulder, like a pioneer
He knows the ax must break a tree
Before we learn the lesson of light,
Like a fisherman, he knows
The rhythms of water, the shattering
Of moonlight on the shore,
The uses of calm and of silence.

What I remember best, Homer said,
Is the smell of paint, his hand
Moves like a shark or a whip,
His eyes like a knife, cutting away,
Narrow as an oriental's, moving
Like palm leaves in a hot wind,
Fill my pipe for me, he said,
His eyes like a fox in deep snow,
His hand steady as a crow,
I'm too busy to stop.

3. HOPPER

At night the electric light
Makes new shadows and new spaces,

Echoes in the street,
Or in a dark theater in 1939
Where Hopper is watching *Dark Victory*
It separates you from the shadow
And holds you like a still life,
Pensive, alone, alive.

What I wanted to do, Hopper said,
Was to paint sunlight on the side
Of a house, sunlight seen solid,
Sunlight on white walls, on windows,
On a white fence, sunlight
In brick shadows, on brick walls,
Sunlight as blue as an ocean,
As brown as a roof, as solid as sand.

You meet him in Chicago,
Or early Sunday morning in New York,
He is alone on Manhattan Bridge
Or having coffee late at night,
He knows the democracy of light,
Light on a bridge in Manhattan,
Or a bridge breaking pine woods,
On a house by the railroad,
The equality of trees and wood siding,
Light on a lighthouse, or light
On the shoulders of a friend.

Hopper's face is like windows,
You see yourself or a landscape,
The angles of stonework and steel,
The subtleties of water,
The energy of oil, Hopper's face
Is like sunlight, alone and alive.

SHE

(*After the English of Jorge Luis Borges*)

> *In town or field, or by the insatiate sea,*
> *Men brood on buried loves, and unforgot . . .*

— H. Rider Haggard

You want her.
You have little to offer:

Your hour under the moon,
The blue asphalt like steel,
The memory you hold of a smile,
Caught like silver in your eye,
A touch of fingers, her hand
Held out from the window
As she leaves (the last time).

A past: dead men, ghosts,
An odor of verbena, "dying thunder of hooves,"
The charge of three hundred men in Peru,
Your father's father wrapped in the hide of a cow,
A soldier shot at Gettysburg,
Caught among boulders, his leg stiff as leather,
The knife his son fashioned,
Touched now with rust, sharp as an eye.

The expression of your books,
The books themselves, green, orange, gold,
The paper stiff as a knee.

Your loyalty
And the fact of your betrayals.

Yourself, the smile no mirror shows,
Safe from time, from joy, from pain.

A glimpse of a yellow rose
In a goblet by a bed.

Your theories of her:
News that opens like a knife, a window,
Authentic and surprising news.

The loneliness that wakes you late and lonely,
The hunger that wakes you,
The lure of uncertainty, danger,
The possibility of defeat.

HOMAGE TO ERIC AMBLER

Like water oiling the bristled piles,
Rust on a freighter's plates,
Moving like shadows along the dockside,
The thin scratch of a phonograph,
The needle scraping like wool on chafed skin,
The touch of a hand for only a moment,
An echo, an echo, an echo like water.

You stand on the balcony with a slim cigar,
You know too much, your eyes are heavy with it,
You are in fog leaning like a streetlamp,
Like a street, wet and electric,
Aware of common danger, a passage as of arms,
A state of continuing siege, your eyes are heavy,
Like smoke, like fog, like the roll of waters.

The light crackles down mountain walls
So that your hair stands on end, you tighten,
The darkness flees into alleyways,
Under trees, slips under passing cars,
You are tense as a lit fuse, sparks,
A hiss of nerves, you strike a match
With a scrape like needles on the stone wall.

But you have solved it, working alone,
Working with others and no loss of self-respect,
Cracked it like a simple code, notes of a song,
You feel the hand that holds hard, that grips,
Your eyes as narrow as the iris of a lens,
You say the word, the words, like the light
That spreads on water, you see the broken day:

You write it on the walls.

MARCH AGAIN

The stable universe is slipping away
from under us.

— A. N. Whitehead

How the light returns to you,
How even the gray bark of trees
Seems to shed light and the ground
Is as bright and as fluid as air.
How your skin opens like an eye:
You are warm as glass, as clear.

In the evening it snows
And the wind rattles the roof
Like knuckles or bullets,
The curtains puff away
From the closed windows.
You hold to the lamp's circle,
Well away from the wall.
Only blood moves through you
Like light through fog,
You close your eyes
And the room silently moves.

In the morning the wind sharpens
The pond to blades, to light,
Wave on wave on wave.
You grow dizzy and each step
Is like walking on water,
Is like walking on knives.
The wind is around you like a wall.

How you are stirring like a bulb
In soil, you open like an eye,
The lids curled back like lips
In a snarl, how you follow
The shadows of birds, a tatter
As of discarded paper or shavings,
How the day stretches like dogs
And the shadows shrink in the grass.

Christ could have swum away
From the cross on air,
But he chose to be nailed
To the ground. You grow dizzy
And each step is like walking
On water, is like walking on knives.
The ground sheds light like a lamp.
The wind rattles the trees like bones.
Only blood calls you to move
Well away from the walls.

from THINGS TO LOOK AT

for Maeryn Stradley

1.

A shell you found on the beach,
Half covered in sand. It was late evening,
And the sun wavered red and lonely in the slow sea.
You were alone, and the air was as quiet as water.

And, of course, you lost it,
Left it in the corner of the room
Or behind the white pitcher.
Or perhaps you dropped it,
A curl of calcium in the white sand,
Pink and sharp and circling,
As clean as water or white sand.

A shell you found on the beach
And knew it to see. You see
It now and know the edges of the eye,
A line of damp sand, the returning sea.

4.

The way the eager dog,
After he has jumped up to greet you
And wagged his tail out
And bumped his head under your hand
(A pat or quick scratch will do)
More than once, will settle
Like a warm breeze or evening flower,
Perhaps on the red rug by the window
Or against your foot, will stretch out
At length or lower his head (looking up),
Or will lie poised and alert,
His front paws crossed, an X,
And will look you steady eye to eye.

7.

You are by yourself,
Sitting in the grass under a tree,

The shade like a circle around you.
The afternoon is warm and very slow.
You have been thinking how dreams change
When they come to be, how they disappoint
Or simply fade away.

And you see a bright butterfly,
Golden and royal red, like sunlight,
Like the bright center of sunlight,
Touching the white blossoms of clover
And hovering like a stillness of air.

Your dream:
That he will land on your finger,
That if you are still as a blossom
He will settle on your finger,
Will tremble there like light on water,
Like sunlight on rippling water.

But the butterfly fades like a dream,
Like the afternoon, flies out of sight,
Around a bush or into deep shade.
Your mind wanders, you drift
Out of focus.

There is another butterfly,
Dark purple, blue black,
The color of a new bruise,
Dusty and dark, flying from flowers,
Flying to your finger like a drunk,
Weaving, wobbling to his left,
And he lands. You are amazed.

This butterfly will not leave.
He is ugly and strange, he stands
On your finger like a blot.
You brush him away, but he clings
Like a shadow or a stain.
His wings waver like the arms
Of a man balancing on a fence,
But he balances, he stays.
Your dream has entered the day
Like a dark surprise.

The sun is golden and yellow.
Clovers dot the wide green grass.
There is a butterfly on your finger,
Like the cool center of shade,
But he is as warm as sunlight, as steady
As a tidal sea. He remains.
He is like the day that holds you,
The air that wraps you round.
The afternoon lengthens and deepens.
You are sitting in the tree's green shadow.
There is a butterfly on your finger.

You are everything that you could ever wish to be.

EMERSON, POE AND BORGES

> *Incredibly, within twenty seconds, they had left*
> *fire, smoke, their fate and their death behind.*

— Ellery Queen

I

(After the Spanish of Jorge Luis Borges)

The sun draws out the afternoon
As long as its shadow.
You are thinking of Emerson,
How that tall American must have found a day as long,
How he must have closed his book,
His marked copy of Montaigne,
How he must have walked out into the sunlight,
Toward the sunlight, the last sharp edge of the day.
You shape his thoughts
As he walks the wide pampas of your mind:

I have read the books that I must
And written others that will outlast this day.
I have been given all that a man may know.
My name circles the globe,
But I have not lived.
I would be another man.

Then Emerson fades in the dusk.
A bat skips the air by your face
Like a stone.
You turn to go inside.
You think: I have not lived.
I would be another man.

Your face examines you
From the clear glass of your door.

II

(After the Spanish of Jorge Luis Borges)

That night you think of Poe
Who did not fear the night.

You see him carved in black marble,
The ivy inching its way up the stone
Like worms that measure the grave.
Poe never feared earth or the worm:
He only feared the luck of the day,
The luck that gives you love
And takes that love away —
Not the dark stone, but a single yellow rose.

Poe's is the face on the other side of the glass,
There with the nightmares he shaped by hand,
With things and thoughts,
With silence and shadow, the turning rim of the pool.

You think of him on the other side of death:
Alone, silent, strong, making marvels
Both splendid and atrocious.

The wind opens the curtains at your window.
The night is moonless.
You hear the quiet movement of water.

III

The next morning you are Borges:
Borges waking, Borges at breakfast,
Borges walking toward the sunlight,
Borges afoot in the rising dew.

You, too, have made marvels,
Written words that will last,
And you have recognized the face
In the mandala of your lines.

You are in a world of forms,
Shapes of the open day,
They glow like new coins.

You walk as precisely as the edge of a knife,
You are light as air.

You are thinking of two gauchos,
How words echo like the jingle of spurs,

Of what you must say, how you have seen
All that a man may know, how when you reach the curb
You will stop and listen carefully,
And cross the avenue, walk in the formal trees
Until you reach the wide river,
The clear water silent as moving glass.

GETTYSBURG

for Bruce and Betsy Stefany

It don't hurt a bit to be shot in a wooden leg.
— Lt. Gen. Richard S. Ewell, CSA

It is a swelling and falling away of ground,
Stones and stone, the trees lined up along the wall,
And an accumulation of names.

Gettysburg has an echo
Like a shout in rocks.
You hear it
Even when you look away.

Say Spangler's Spring or Culp's Hill,
The Round Tops, the Angle,
Say the Devil's Den,
Say Cemetery Hill.

Fifty thousand hit in July,
Down in Pennsylvania farm dirt.
Richard Dillard felt his leg collapse
With a bright stain like a fallen flag.
Home is just over the hill, they said,
And two years later it was.

We'll fight them, sir, till hell freezes over,
And then, sir, we'll fight them on the ice.

Too bad, Lee said, too bad.
Oh, too bad. And then the rain
Slid down the butts of rifles,
Down the barrels and bayonet blades
And into the ground, the first drops
Dancing in the dust like live things,
Then a rush that laid all dust to rest.

The real war was somewhere to the west.
This one was only a dream, a spring
Of dreams, dreams that still splash
Like living things on the ground.

It is ground and grass,
A piling up of names like stones,
It is earth and air, a place to live.
You can move through echoes without a glance
Or drop them like postcards into the box
To be sent on with best wishes.

Or you can walk out Wainwright Avenue,
Past Hancock on his horse, and Slocum,
Slowly, thinking of another day, other days,
Watch the high clouds circle like birds
And hold hands or not this day, as you will.

You feel the muscles in your legs
Climbing Culp's Hill, climbing the tower
On Culp's Hill, feel the blood moving
In them like slow ice or warm as plowed ground.
Names fade in this accumulation of air.
You can see the day turn through the clouds.

If you need to remember anything,
It is the best way home.

LIMITS

(After the Spanish of Jorge Luis Borges)

The rain holds you in like skin
Or a wall, steady, almost solid.
The brick walls through the trees
Move like dreams or memories.
Your eyes search for sharp things,
Objects with edges, lights like knives.
The day has lost all definition,
Is as closed as some dark lithograph.

You remember:
The rain of May, the rain of July,
The rain of ten years ago in the winter,
A whisper shared in the rain,
How the rain smashes on your shoes
Or its loose rattle on an umbrella,
Rain in weeds or across water,
The taste of rain, the smell,
How her skin is as slick and shiny
In the rain as an apple or plums.

You know:
There is a poem by Borges
You will never remember,
And a street (it curves down the hill)
That is forever closed to you,
At least one door (the knob once warm
With your hand) which you have closed
Until the end of the world.

I know a face which I seek in every stranger's,
Which I shall never see again.
I know there are books in my shelves
(They are all around me now)
Which I shall never open again.
This wet autumn closes my thirty-fourth year.
Death continues to blur and reduce me,
To reduce you as you read this page,
Steadily and as sure as rain.

SURPRISES

We cannot stay among the ruins.

— R. W. Emerson

The sudden edge of a bell
Or a knock. You answer,
If at all, touching wood.

You touch wood, and you answer.
It is like turning a page.
It is the mailman or a boy.
It is the undertaker.
It is Cyndy whom you haven't seen for months
Or Cronan who was just by yesterday.
It is a pirate with someone on his shoulder,
Someone you know.

The day dazzles, dances,
The light splashing in like rain.
There are twelve policemen at your door.
There are two men with a cow
Or one man with an eye like a radish.

There is no one at the door at all.

No point in going back to bed.
The day is torn open like an envelope.
It is as open as the door.
You are opening like a door,
Steadying like a zeppelin in the air.
You take on edges. You expand.

Something has come to call
And found you in. And now
You must go calling on the day.

AFTER BORGES

*No force of imagination can convert us into
another person, and make us fancy, that we,
being that person, reap benefit from those
valuable qualities, which belong to him. Or
if it did, no celerity of imagination could
immediately transport us back, into ourselves,
and make us love and esteem the person, as
different from us.*

— David Hume

These things we share:
Sun, water, earth,
The primary need of air,
The round rhythm of day on day.

These things we gain:
A dream of fire, of a tiger's eye,
The salt desert's glare,
A wisdom of the silent south,
The last labyrinth's one straight line,
Windows, doors, the winding paths
That lead to an open way.

These things we need:
Secrets of Welsh stone in Wiltshire,
Of winds at Egyptian sunset,
Of the reach of grasses at dawn
And sources of shadow at noon,
The strength to walk on water,
The gift of breathing in,
Faith of breathing out,
Fact of the waiting world.

These things we are:
All things, one thing distinct
And nothing more, Borges and I
As different as day from day,
A meeting, a turning away,
Surprise and its sudden result,
A river that flows on to stay.

CODA

SOME NOTES ON A BASSOON

for George Garrett
on his fiftieth birthday

The unexamined life, that gift
Like the first vibration from lip
To tooth to hollow bone to skull.

The unexplained life, that truth
Like tentative scales, the tuning,
The windy hop from note to note to note.

The unexcluding life, that joy
Like the fingered air of the opening movement,
The long and varied middle, the pause at the end.

The unending life, that promise
Like a startling coda, leap ahead,
Music like light, like music in the eye.

Typography by Donald M. Henriksen, Scholarly Typography
Jacket and title page art by Bailey-Montague & Assoc.